HOT STOCK MARKET STRATEGIES

5 SECRET SHORT-TERM TRADING STRATEGIES THAT WORK IN A BULL OR BEAR MARKET

JACOB BER

EP
Entrepreneur. Press

Managing editor: Jere L. Calmes
Cover design: Pay-Fan
Composition and production: Eliot House Productions

This publication is designed to provide accurate and authoritative information in regard to the subject matter covered. It is sold with the understanding that the publisher is not engaged in rendering legal, accounting, or other professional services. If legal advice or other expert assistance is required, the services of a competent professional person should be sought.

Library of Congress Cataloging-in-Publication Data

Bernstein, Jacob, 1946-

    Hot stock market strategies: 5 secret short term trading strategies that work in a bull or bear market/by Jake Bernstein.

    p.   cm.

    Includes index.   MAR '07
    ISBN 1-932531-25-4

    1. Stocks. 2. Speculation. 3. Investment analysis. I. Title.

HG4661.B462 2005

332.63'22—dc22   2004061986

Printed in Canada

10 09 08 07 06 05   10 9 8 7 6 5 4 3 2

Contents

Chapter 6
Gap Your Way to Profits 71

Chapter 7
Short-Term Key Date Seasonal Trades 99

Chapter 8
Day-of-Week Patterns in the Stock Market 141

Chapter 9
Surfing the Stock Channel 153

Chapter 10
Discipline and Trader Psychology 167

Acknowledgments

I extend heartfelt thanks to those who assisted me in the research, writing and editing of this book. Specifically, I wish to thank the following:

- My wife, Linda, for her constant patience with me
- My three wonderful children, who have been supportive and encouraging during the writing of yet another book about trading
- My ever helpful and wonderfully capable associate, Marilyn Kinney for keeping me on track during this time-consuming process
- Bi Hui Lin, my office assistant, for helping me remain organized and on schedule
- The fantastic people at Genesis Financial Data (gfds.com), for allowing me to use charts, systems, and market histories from their Navigator Platinum charting software

- Mark Shriver, programmer extraordinaire who wrote the computer code for many of the systems I have taught you in this book
- Dr. Richard Smith, for his programming of my High Odds Seasonal Trades (HOST) and www.seasonaltrader.com
- Linda Konner my literary agent, for helping me sell this book
- Jere Calmes of Entrepreneur Press for giving me the opportunity to make my good methods known to serious traders all over the world
- My clients, subscribers, and students throughout the world, who have been supportive over the years
- Finally, I would like to extend special thanks to Karen Billipp of Eliot House for her professional and thorough editing of my manuscript. It was my pleasure to have worked with her.

Preface

This book is about making money in the stock market.

This book is not about economics.

This book is not about theory.

This book is not about forecasting prices or trends.

This book will not teach you how to invest for the long term.

This book will not tell you how to manage your retirement funds.

This book will teach you five highly effective short-term trading strategies.

This book will show you moneymaking short-term trading methods in stocks.

This book will help you determine if short-term stock trading is right for you.

This book will debunk several popular market myths.

This book will help you get started on the right track to short-term stock profits.

This book could very well change your financial life for the better.

More specifically, this book is about trading for short-term profits in the stock market using five precise methods that I have developed during my many years in the stock and commodity markets. I will not attempt to turn you into a financial wizard or a market guru. I will simply present you with methods that have the potential to make you a goodly sum of money IF you have the discipline and motivation to use them consistently.

Before we begin, however, I must get a few housekeeping details out of the way.

▶ Trading versus Investing

There has been much controversy among market experts as to the differences between trading and investing. Investors have been characterized as stable, serious, financially well-off types who are focused on implementing the capitalist ideal by using their money to make money over the long term. By long term, I mean a period of more than six months. Indeed, in today's changing economic environment, the definition of long term is very different than it was prior to the late 1980s. In those days investors held stocks for a number of years in order to achieve slow and steady gains. There was nothing wrong with that strategy and there is still nothing wrong with it, if you have time and considerable patience.

For those who are less willing to wait from two to seven years for results, there are many short-term opportunities in today's markets. The short-term end of the market does not necessarily mean "day-trading" (i.e., trading within the time frame of the day and not keeping stocks overnight). These opportunities were created by increased stock market volatility that began in the 1990s. By "volatility," I mean relatively large price movements in stocks during the course of the trading day.

As the stock market soared ever higher into the late 1990s, these large price moves within the trading day created even more opportunities for those who sought to take advantage of these relatively large moves. Brokerage houses, the media, newsletters, and advisory services all jumped on the day-trading bandwagon. Day trading was the new game in town. I jumped on that bandwagon as well, authoring three widely read books on day trading (two on the futures markets and one on the stock market). For several years day trading captured the spotlight.

As the markets continued to "jump," I was slowly but surely overtaken by the thought that the day-trading frenzy might be coming to an end. This premonition was reinforced while I was on a trip to New York City. I hailed a taxi to get back to my hotel after a television appearance. Upon entering the cab I noticed that the driver had a laptop computer on the seat next to him. I could barely believe my eyes when I saw what appeared to be a chart of a stock on the screen of his computer. Below the chart was a quote board of stock prices showing real-time quotes. Not being one to pry, I sat back while he inched his way through the traffic with one eye on the road, the other eye on the screen. Several minutes into the trip he placed a call on his cell phone. Was it the taxi company dispatcher he called? Was it his family? Was it a friend? No, it was his broker! He was actually day trading stocks from his taxi. At that precise moment I knew that things were about to change. Although I can't recall what exact thoughts were running through my mind, the scene was a peculiar one indeed. Here I was in a New York taxi that was being piloted by a turban-wearing, bearded East Indian gentleman who spoke only limited English but who was day trading stocks from his cab using his cell phone and a wireless laptop computer!

Indeed, the game did change. From 2000 through early 2004, stocks became less volatile and with the decrease in volatility, day trading opportunities diminished. On the other hand, short-term trading opportunities continued to be plentiful. By short term I mean from two to about ten day's duration. As brokerage house commissions for online trading continued to decline, the cost of trading decreased, thereby making short-term as well as day trading more viable. This book will show you four specific short-term trading strategies and one specific day trading strategy. While I believe that day-trading can be profitable, it is an arduous venture that is both time-consuming, labor-intensive, and often not worth the time or trouble unless you are totally dedicated and willing to trade a large number of shares each time.

▶ Making Money in the Market Ain't so Easy Any More

For most independent investors, winning in the stock market is not nearly as easy as it used to be. Big traders, money managers, insiders, and other professional traders keep getting smarter, trickier, and faster. Some of them engage in illegal and/or unethical practices, all designed to separate you from your hard-earned money. They do all it takes to line their pockets. While it's true that not all professionals are involved in these games, there are enough unscrupulous individuals out there to make a difference in your bottom line.

Whether market professionals are honest or not is not a major issue. We take for granted that there are all sorts of shenanigans, quasi-legal, unethical, or downright illegal schemes whose sole purpose is to screw the average investors out of their money. The "good old boys" network is alive and thriving. It will always be with us no matter how aggressively the authorities attempt to eliminate its evils. The "greed machine" is a constant. It feeds on the public as grist for the mill. But let's face it: the public is an easy target, ripe for the picking.

The vast majority of investors have no idea what they're doing and continue to pour money down the sewer hole. While this is true in stocks and options, it is even more prevalent in the commodity futures and options markets. The unfortunate irony is that when small investors lose money they cry foul, point the finger at money managers and/or brokers, and hire gunslinger lawyers to get them settlements. It's a nasty system that, although biased against the little guy, also claims innocent professionals as victims.

The numerous scandals that have been discovered since the mid 1990s are likely only the tip of the iceberg. There are many tricks and questionable practices that remain pervasive in the markets. But this book is not about any of that. I am not a muckraker. This book is about one thing and one thing only: it's about how to kick ass in the stock market without getting your ass kicked, no matter how biased the system may be against you.

If my direct, perhaps blunt statements are offensive to you then perhaps you may want to grow a thicker skin or get your winning market strategies from another market analyst who will sugarcoat things for you. There are plenty of those around. No, I won't tell you only what you want to hear; I won't cater to you; I won't tell you that everything is for the best in the best of all possible worlds. I don't care who I offend. I have many enemies in the financial world who would love to see my demise. What they hate most about me is that I'll tell you how things really are, even if I have to step on some pretty high-up toes.

With over 35 years of market experience behind me I haven't the time, the patience, or the interest in feeding you a line of idealistic BS that gives you hope but no profits. Forget about hope. Forget about idealism. Forget about what should or should not be! It's time to face the facts and, moreover, to use the markets to our advantage no matter how flawed or corrupt the system may be.

In closing, I add that corruption in the markets is here to stay. Now that electronic trading has come of age, you can expect a plethora of high-tech scams. White-collar financial criminals have now added computers to their bag of tricks. I suspect that in the next few years we will see a number of new frauds, all designed to rip off the average investor as well as some of the biggest financial institutions in the world. The cops and robbers, good guys vs. bad guys game will continue. In order to avoid being caught in the crossfire you will need to have the right strategies and tools, and you will need to implement defensive strategies. First, however, you will need a solid base or structure from which to operate. While some of you may consider the next chapter to be boring or perhaps even unnecessary, I urge you to read it, to study it, and to make it an integral part of all of your investment strategies.

If there is only one gift I can give you, if there is only one thing I can teach you in this book, if there is only one lasting achievement that this book can help you realize, then the next two chapters will take you there. Accordingly, I ask you not to skip the next two chapters, even if you believe yourself to be a highly accomplished investor or trader. If you have been losing money in the markets, if you have been making money in the markets (but not enough of it), if you have the feeling that something is missing from your trading or investing strategy, or if you're a newcomer to the markets, then the next two chapters could very well change your results for the better—and forever.

CHAPTER

1

General Investment Model (GIM)

An Overview

 As noted at the end of the Introduction, this chapter will provide you with the quintessential structure to a trading or investing approach that has the potential to help you realize your goals of success in the markets, and the financial independence that accompanies it. As you will discover later in this book, I am a firm believer in the importance of organization, discipline, effective investor psychology, and thorough planning of your trades and financial decisions. If your goal is to achieve consistent success as

a trader, or even as an investor, you will need to follow the rules and strategies discussed in this book. On the other hand, if you are not a serious trader, if you want to use the stock market as a casino, then you don't need this book and you don't need to waste your time reading any further.

▶ Introduction to the General Investment Model (GIM)

The investment model you will learn in this chapter is the first of two vital steps that form the underlying structure of profitable investing. Simply learning this model will *not* guarantee success. You will need to internalize it, apply it, and study it until it becomes second nature to you. The General Investment Model (GIM) will help you understand investing in general; however, understanding something and knowing *how* to actually put it into practice profitably, are two very different things.

While I may be overstating the importance of the GIM, I will take that risk in order to drive my point home. I firmly believe that unless you follow the GIM and the implementation strategy described in the next chapter, your success in the stock market may be limited, spotty, or, at best, questionable. I sincerely believe that this chapter and the next can open your eyes to a new and highly structured trading approach that may well become the basis of all investment decisions you will make in virtually any field. If you do nothing else with this book, I ask you to make a commitment to learn and put into practice the general investment approach and method discussed in this chapter and the next.

If you have been led to believe that success in the markets is merely a matter of picking the right stocks, you have been given only half the truth. There is much more to the process than simply making the right stock selections. Not only do you need to pick the right stocks at the right time, but you also need to implement your buying and selling strategies correctly, while managing the risks and maximizing the profits. The GIM and the implementation strategy will complete the equation for you. By then applying the five winning strategies discussed in later chapters, you will have the complete package for successful trading.

▶ The First Step

The GIM provides an underlying structure or model that I have developed from my many years of experience in the markets as a trader, investor, teacher, analyst, researcher, and systems developer. Don't let the title of this model intimidate you! The GIM is a very simple concept. It is easy to understand and perhaps even enjoyable to apply. I have found that some individuals are so thrilled with what the GIM does, that they follow it in other areas of their lives.

The GIM is a practical, sensible, and basic approach that overcomes the disorganization, myth, misinformation, and disinformation that have hindered investor success for all too many years. If you consider interpersonal relationships to be investments of a sort, then you may find this model useful in your personal life as well. As you well know, structure is vital to success in any field of endeavor. Without structure, you will merely be stabbing at opportunities without the necessary knowledge, direction, or tools.

From time to time you will hit a few profitable trades, but your overall track record will be abysmal. Unless you are one of the fortunate few whose psychic or perceptive abilities are highly developed, you will forever be relegated to the ranks of the market losers.

The first step is to rid yourself of bad learning that may be standing in the way of your success. Clear the myths and worthless methods from your mind and repertoire. Try something new and effective for a change! Use the GIM.

I consider the GIM to be the first step in any investing program. This holds true if you plan to make only one trade or a thousand trades. Before you reach any trading decision you MUST view it

.05 +1.3	BL		InITE	9.69	+.04 +2.1	IM		FF2010n	13.12	-.07 +1.4	BL		FndofAmY	25.20	-.14 +5.0	MC		MySecs
.03 +2.5	IL		Mgdin	9.35	+.02 +4.0	AB		FF2020n	13.07	-.11 +1.0	XC		GlobalA	35.41	+.07 +6.3	GL		SmlCapGr
.09 +.9	BL		STGvSec	7.11	+.1.1	SU		FF2030n	12.99	-.14 +.5	XC		OverseasA	19.59	+.04 +7.8	IL		SmallCo
.10 +.3	XC											SoGenGold	15.85	+.55 -9.0	ALL		USGovSec

within the GIM framework. As noted above, unless you are very lucky, psychic, or privy to solid inside information, you will not be able to make money or have a successful *relationship* with your investments without an investing model like the GIM.

The GIM is only one of several investment approaches that can help you achieve consistent success. I favor this method above all others, because it is simple to understand, easily applied to all types of investments, historically valid, and totally logical.

Different Points of View

Although some investors and/or market professionals will disagree vehemently with my emphasis on the GIM, I believe that it has opened the eyes of thousands of investors who have been the fortunate recipients of my knowledge, whether in my books, speaking engagements, or seminars. Once you learn the GIM, you will be able to determine where you may have gone astray with some of your previous investments and trades, and you will find out what you did that was right. Accordingly, the GIM will help you avoid repetitive errors, while at the same time allowing you to maximize your profits.

Unless you learn and internalize the GIM, the five highly effective tools discussed in this book will be useless. Some market professionals argue that a good method of stock selection is all that is necessary for success. If you have not already discovered that they are wrong, then you surely will see once you have learned the GIM and the implementation strategy.

▶ The Five-Part GIM Structure

The GIM consists of five parts, or aspects:

    1. *Historical pattern*. The identification of specific patterns that have shown a tendency to repeat themselves a high percentage of the time.

2. *Expectation*. What we anticipate or expect a market or stock to do in the future, based on its established historical pattern(s).

3. *Confirmation*. Tools used to increase the probability of an expectation becoming a reality.

4. *Action*. Specific market entry and exit strategies and methods designed to put the first three steps into action.

5. *Money management*. Detailed procedures to minimize risk and maximize profits once steps one through five have been put into place.

While this model may not have much sex appeal, it does give valuable information and perspective to every investment. Each aspect or step in the GIM depends on the successful and thorough application and understanding of the previous step. If any step in the model is skipped or incorrectly applied, the model will fail and you will most likely lose money. On the other hand, if you correctly follow each step, your odds of making money are considerably higher than if you had not used the GIM. While you may still lose

FIGURE 1.1 General Investment Method Flow Chart

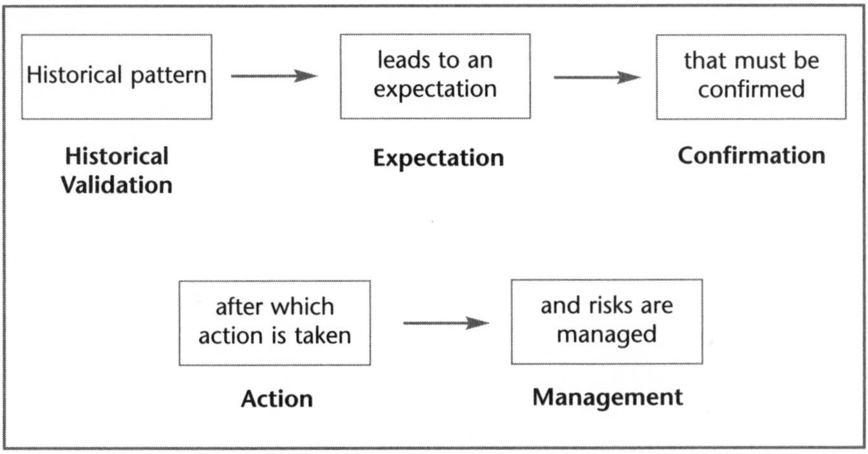

| Historical pattern | → | leads to an expectation | → | that must be confirmed |

Historical Validation **Expectation** **Confirmation**

| after which action is taken | → | and risks are managed |

Action **Management**

money, your overall success should improve markedly. There are no guarantees, because investing and trading are, to a given extent, dependent upon probabilities and are necessarily limited by some of the random behavior that is always inherent in the financial markets.

How the GIM Works

Now let's take a look at the specific steps and aspects of the GIM. Remember to keep an open mind and focus on the logic of what I'm saying and *not* on the ultimate goal. The goal will take care of itself if your understanding and application are correct. Earlier in this chapter I asked you to free your mind of what you may have learned elsewhere, because much of it may be worthless, pointless, misguided, and/or market myth. I remind you again to please do so in studying what follows.

Phase 1: The Historical Pattern

All investment and trading decisions must be based, to a given extent, on an historical pattern. They must be based on facts that have historical validity. Simply stated, they must have a valid basis as opposed to a decision made on random facts, coincidence, rumor, promises, wishes, or unfounded expectations. The bad news about historical patterns is that millions of investors believe historical patterns that are either incorrect or not based on the actual facts. The good news about historical patterns is that there are indeed many whose validity is demonstrable as well as profitable, when and if used correctly.

What exactly is an historical pattern? The simple answer is that each investment area, stock, financial market, real estate, business and interpersonal relationship has a pattern. What is a pattern? A pattern is a series of events or relationships that has a history of repetition. An event becomes a pattern by virtue of its repetitive history. There are literally hundreds of patterns in our daily lives and in the financial markets. In the markets these patterns consist of repetitive price cycles, seasonality, chart patterns, earnings reports, day-of-week relationships, and market indicators. As a trader, you will want to follow the most effective patterns. As an example of what I mean by a pattern consider the cyclical pattern in the price of natural gas as shown in Figure 1.2.

FIGURE 1.2 ▶ Three- to Four-Year Cycles in Natural Gas Prices

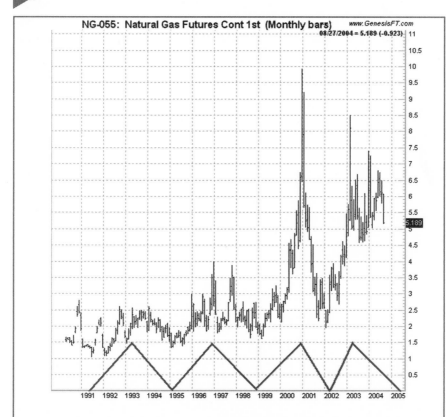

This chart shows the fluctuations in gas patterns since prior to 1991. While the history is clear and highly repetitive, there is no assurance that this pattern will continue to be predictable. The chart shows my projection into 2005. Because the historical pattern is not perfect, we use it merely to form an expectation which must then be confirmed by what I call a trigger. The trigger will be discussed in more detail later.

The chart shows the approximate three- to four-year cyclical pattern in the price of natural gas. As you can see, this pattern has run about three to four years in length from one price low to another. Although the price of natural gas does not follow the pattern perfectly, it does track quite closely. The use of a pattern is to help you get close to a turning point in the market. Patterns help you to develop an expectation. It is entirely possible that your expectation will change as time passes. This cyclical pattern, for example, can be used to determine the appropriateness of purchases and sales in natural gas stocks. But bear in mind that expectations are not realities. According to our model, expectations based on historical patterns need to be confirmed or validated before you take action. We do not take action until an expectation is confirmed or "triggered."

If you know how to translate your expectation into action, you will fare well; however, if you allow the expectation to overcome your good judgment, and you make an investment without taking the next step in the GIM, you will probably lose money on your investment. This is a very important point! Please remember it.

Phase 2: Expectation

An expectation based on historical patterns is NOT a reality. It does NOT tell you to enter a trade. It merely points you in a given direction, telling you what MIGHT happen. Never let your expectation of what MIGHT happen become transformed into the belief that it WILL happen. The outcome of an investment or a trade is never a certainty, and as long as you remember this, you will do well. All historical patterns lead us to expectations. Expectations must be confirmed before they can be translated into market actions.

Remember that the majority of investment and trading decisions are made on a limited amount of information. Most investors make their decisions based only on historical expectations. They do not wait for expectations to be confirmed by reality. In my experience, when many investors and traders go astray they fail to wait for indications that their expectations based on history are likely to develop into realities. Note that even when we confirm an expectation, there is still a good element of chance in the markets. It is therefore possible that although we may have been attentive, diligent, and thorough in waiting for a market to confirm historical expectations, we may still lose money. The goal is to be wrong as little as possible. The methods in this book, in particular the GIM and the Setup, Trigger, and Follow-Through (STF), to follow in the next chapter, are designed to keep you on the winning side much more often than on the losing side.

In the example cited earlier for natural gas, the historical pattern of a three- to four-year cycle is translated as an expectation that the market will bottom or top in a given time frame. This expectation alone is not sufficient to result in an investment. As you will see in the STF method, the entire procedure follows in a step-by-step sequence that will help you plan your trades and trade your plans. The most important aspect of following a set procedure is that if you make a mistake, you will be able to track your effort(s) to see where you went wrong. And from this process you will learn from every mistake.

Historical Patterns Lead to Expectations

If you allow your expectation to influence you to the point of believing that it MUST become a reality, then you are headed for losses and trouble. As an example, consider the attitudes of most investors with regard to the gold market. Many investors believe that gold is the right investment to make in the event of political or economic instability. The idea that gold might be a good protective investment in such cases is correct. It has been validated time and time again by actual historical facts. It is based on historical precedent. However, the facts also suggest that for many years gold has been a relatively poor investment. Many investors, nonetheless, believe that whenever an international situation threatens to escalate or when inflation seems imminent, their best financial strategy is a defensive one. They believe that in such instances it is best to buy gold-mining stocks, or gold in the form of coins or even bullion.

Although their expectation, based on historical precedent, is an accurate and reasonable one, they are not always correct. While their reasoning is soundly based on what HAS happened, it is also based on the erroneous belief that international conflict or financial crises always (or most often) cause the price of gold to rise. In actuality, this is *not* correct. Situations are rarely that simple. The relationship between conflict, economic instability, inflation or deflation, and the price of gold is not 100 percent predictable. However, it may be correct a good 70 percent of the time.

When investors buy gold in anticipation of a crisis, and the price of gold fails to go up when the crisis actually develops, the only reasonable action is to get out of gold because the expectation, based on a historical belief, failed to develop into a reality. But problems arise when investors, especially in gold, refuse to exit their failed investment when their expectation does not materialize. They hold on to their gold investment as it declines over days, months, and even years. They allow the market to "hold their investment hostage" as they keep their capital tied up in a nonproductive investment because they are convinced that their expectations will eventually become reality. But gold is not unique in this respect. This is typical investor behavior no matter what market or stock is involved. The end result of such behavior is that when the expectation fails to materialize after many days, weeks, or months, investors often give up in despair very close to the end of the move.

The Y2K Folly

The gold example is only one very small illustration of what occurs when investors allow their expectations to influence their thoughts and actions. Another more glaring example of such a situation was

5 +1.3	BL	IntTE	9.69	+.04 +2.1	IM	FF2010n	13.12	-.07 +1.4	BL	FndotAmY	25.20	-.14 +5.0	MC	MigSecs
3 +2.5	IL	Mgdln	9.35	+.02 +4.0	AB	FF2020n	13.07	-.11 +1.0	XC	GlobalA	35.41	+.07 +6.3	GL	SmlCapGro 1
9 +.9	BL	STGvSec	7.11	+1.1	SU	FF2030n	12.99	-.14 +.5	XC	OverseasA	19.59	+.04 +7.8	IL	SmallCo 1
0 +.3	XC									SoGenGoldn15.85		+.55 -.90	ALI	USGovSecs 1

the Y2K bug and the "end of the world" hysteria that accompanied the coming of the 21st century. You may recall that many "knowledgeable" and respected politicians, scientists, economists, financial advisors, and clergypersons warned us of what might happen. Many individuals in positions of authority acted responsibly and sensibly to avoid alarming the public.

Others, however, were quite vocal in their fear campaign. Some of these alarmists told investors to sell their stocks and to stockpile food, medical supplies, fuel, batteries, and weapons. These astounding and dire predictions seem laughable now that we look back on them. But while they may seem comical to us, some people actually believed them and made major preparations.

Sadly enough, it is very likely that some frightened people actually sold their homes, stockpiled supplies, liquidated their investments, and closed their bank accounts. The century came and went with virtually no problems. Those who acted without confirmation of their expectations were not only made to feel like fools, but also lost money and their investment positions. This was a classic example of mass hysteria promoted by belief in an expectation that was both unfounded in historical precedent and not confirmed by actual events. In short, the Y2K panic was a fiasco that will be cited many times in the history books as an example of investor hysteria.

Phase 3: Confirmation of Historical Expectations

The next step is to confirm an expectation. There are many methods for confirming expectations. Another word for these is "timing." Technical traders use market-timing indicators to validate or confirm an expectation. Once we have formulated an expectation based on historically valid patterns, we must have a method by which we verify or confirm that the given expectation is highly likely to become a reality. We need a method by which to tilt the odds in our favor. These methods will be discussed in Chapters 5 through 9.

.05 +1.3	BL		IntTE	9.69	+.04 +2.1	IM		FF2010n	13.12	−.07 +1.4	BL		FndofAmY	25.20	−.14 +5.0	MC		MySec
.03 +2.5	L		Mgdln	9.35	+.02 +4.0	AB		FF2020n	13.07	−.11 +1.0	XC		GlobalA	35.41	+.07 +6.3	GL		SmlCapGr
.09 +.9	BL		STGvSec	7.11	+1.1	SU		FF2030n	12.99	−.14 +.5	XC		OverseasA	19.59	+.04 +7.8	IL		SmallCo
.10 +.3	XC												SoGenGoldnt	5.85	+.55 −9.0	ALL		USGovSec

Phase 4: Action

Once a trade or investment has passed the test of historical validity, thereby creating an expectation that must be triggered, yet another step must be taken. Once triggered or confirmed, the expectation must be put into action. Unfortunately, this is where many investors and traders go astray. For a variety of reasons, they are either unable to take action or they take action too late. The issues here are more psychological and behavioral than they are a function of market behavior. Some of these issues are addressed more fully in Chapters 5 through 9.

It is obvious that without action, nothing will happen. While it's true that you can't lose money if you fail to take action, it's also true that you won't make money if you don't take action. This step in the sequence of the GIM is one of the most critically important, because, as noted earlier, it is in taking action or failing to do so where many investors blunder.

Although taking action sounds like a relatively simple behavior, it is in reality, highly complex, because it dredges up a host of psychological issues that each of us, to a greater or lesser extent, carries with us. We know that psychology is the weakest link in the chain. The process of taking action is, in fact, so intricate and subject to so many potential errors that entire books have been written on the topic. Here are the major issues involved in taking action:

- Why do many investors fail to take action even though they have a valid historical pattern that has been confirmed by a trigger?
- Why do many investors take action either too soon or too late?
- Why do many traders allow others to influence their decisions in spite of historical expectations and confirmation to the contrary?
- Why do so many traders have difficulty getting into or out of an investment after they have followed through with consistency and accuracy?

- What is it that creates the fear that prevents so many investors and traders from taking the appropriate actions at the appropriate times?
- What is it that creates the greed that causes so many investors to take action too soon in spite of the clear rules that they have been given?
- Why do investors become overly aggressive, taking on too much risk?
- Why do investors become meek, timid, or fearful, thereby avoiding trades or investments that are dictated by their own good rules?
- Why do investors allow emotions to influence their decisions even though these emotions are contrary to the logic of their trading methodologies?

Without a doubt, taking action is an integral aspect of the GIM, one that is rarely given sufficient attention in most books, seminars, or courses on investing. Failure to take action, taking improper action, or taking action too soon or too late is the weakest link in the investment chain. Far too many market analysts and trading advisors believe that people will follow through and take action according to the plan. Reality, however, teaches us that this is not the case. I have learned through many years of experience that people don't follow through. *We know without a doubt that even the best methods of investing will become losing propositions if investors fail to take action, take incorrect action in spite of valid information analysis, or somehow alter the course of action.*

Phase 5: Management of Risk and Profit

If you correctly implement the first four parts of the GIM, you will likely increase considerably your odds of making a profit. But simply following the first four steps does not ensure a profit. Nor does it ensure that you won't take a large loss. In order to win at this game you must manage your profits effectively (i.e., maximize them), and you must limit your losses consistently (i.e., minimize them).

You can manage your profits by either turning the paper profit into an actual profit or by holding on to the investment and setting up new possibilities or alternatives based on how the investment continues to perform. If your investment shows a loss, you need to manage the loss by not allowing it to become so large as to either deplete all your available capital, or tie up your money indefinitely while you wait for the loss to become smaller, or even turn into a profit.

Here are the key issues in this portion of the GIM

- When should you take your profit?
- When should you take your loss?
- How much loss is acceptable?
- How much profit should you anticipate?
- When should you add to your investment positions?
- How can you prevent a profit from turning into a loss?
- How long should you wait for a loss to turn into a profit?
- When and how do you know that you made a wrong decision?

The Setup, Trigger, and Follow-Through procedure discussed in the next chapter will give you specific answers to these very valid questions. To a large extent the answers to these questions are a function of the trading methodology you are using. Because this book will teach you five different methods, each method will have different answers to these questions.

▶ Effective Implementation of the GIM

Using the GIM correctly will require discipline, practice, and consistency. The methods you will learn in this book are effective, but their performance will be determined by your ability to follow the GIM and the STF. Here are some general guidelines to assist you in this process.

1. *Determine how much money you can risk as your available trading capital.* Remember that this book is about trading as opposed to investing. As a result, what you will learn is speculative, as opposed to investment-oriented. This does not mean that the GIM will not work for investors. As a matter of fact, it will work exceptionally well. The psychology of the short-term trader is different from that of the investor. There is more risk, more reward, and more volatility. Be prepared for all of these by risking only what you can afford.

2. *Determine whether short-term trading is the right thing for you.* Clearly, someone who has only $500 in risk capital cannot realistically expect to make a great deal of money immediately. Beginning with such a small amount will definitely decrease your odds of success, and it will also limit the number of times you can afford to be wrong before you are knocked out of the game. If you don't have enough money to be a short-term stock market trader, don't play the game. Given market conditions in 2004, I recommend that at least $5,000 in starting capital for short-term stock trading be made available.

3. *Get started.* As you know from my discussion on the preceding pages, I am a strong advocate of action. While you may know that you want to be a trader, you may be hesitant to begin. Even though you may be well-versed in the methods you will learn in this book, you may still be unsure of yourself or insecure about your skills. You will never overcome your limitations if you avoid taking action! Again, I emphasize that action is one of the major keys to success. You need to take action not only when you are actually trading; you also need to take action in order to begin your adventure(s) in trading.

4. *Accept change.* If you're like most investors, you have acquired some bad habits and faulty learning along the way.

Unfortunately, you may have been the victim of market myths (described earlier in this book), or you may be plodding along using methods and systems that just don't work. It's time to make a change! Give the methods in this book time to work. Take time to track them in the market and increase your confidence in them. But don't wait too long to take action. Once you are confident that these markets will work for you, go to step 3, above.

2

Setup, Trigger, and Follow-Through (STF)

And now the fun begins! This chapter will teach you the Setup, Trigger, and Follow-Through (STF) method for implementing your trades. I believe that this chapter can change your investment life forever—and for the better. Once you have learned the STF, you will realize the beauty of its simplicity. If there is only one thing I can teach you in this book, it is the value and implementation of the STF.

I have already discussed the importance of following a defini-tive investment structure such as the GIM. The GIM is an impor-tant tool as it provides a basis or framework for making decisions and evaluating potential trades or investments. The GIM applies to all investments, whether stocks, mutual funds, futures, options, or real estate. The concept is simple but incredibly powerful. If you learn to apply the GIM and STF, they will serve you profitably. Ignore them, and eventually you will return to them as you come to appreciate their logic and efficacy.

You will recall from the previous chapter that I emphasized the importance of avoiding the pitfall of equating expectations with reality. Simply stated, the mere fact that you expect something to happen does not mean it *will* happen. *This is a significant distinction to be given serious consideration at all times.* Do not make the mistake that so many investors make by allowing an expectation to take on the role of a reality, unless the expectation is confirmed or validated by actual events or other methods, which you will learn as you continue reading. I realize that I have made this point many times in the last two chapters, but I would rather err on the side of redun-dancy than on the side of understating the importance of this fact.

▶ The Setup, Trigger, and Follow-Through Approach (STF)

STF is a three-step process that allows you to implement your trad-ing decisions consistently and effectively. Unless you use the STF approach, you will likely be disorganized and random in your trading procedures. The STF approach is applicable to any type of investment.

Here are several examples of the STF approach that I believe will help you understand it more clearly. Once you understand the STF method, you will see trading and investing in a new light. I believe this highly structured approach will make a significant and positive difference in your results.

▶ The STF in Detail

Without a formal set of procedures that control the decision-making process, you will be like every other aspiring investor—a ship at sea without a captain or a course. By following the GIM and the STF methods, you'll have won more than 75 percent of the battle for investment success. Now let's examine the STF in detail. The STF model I would like you to visualize and memorize is shown in Figure 2.1 If you take the time to study this model and apply it to every investment decision you make, it will serve you well. Now let's take a look at a few real-life examples of how the STF model translates into investment action and success.

The historical pattern is shown in Figure 2.2.

The next step is to confirm this trade with a TRIGGER. For this purpose I have used a technical indicator to see if the trade has potential to make money this year as it has done so many times in the past. Figure 2.3 is the chart for DIS, with my indicator and notes.

FIGURE 2.1 ▶ The STF Model

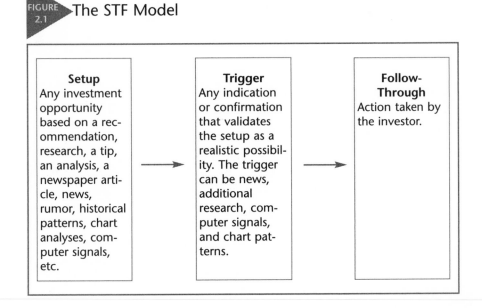

Setup	Trigger	Follow-Through
Any investment opportunity based on a recommendation, research, a tip, an analysis, a newspaper article, news, rumor, historical patterns, chart analyses, computer signals, etc.	Any indication or confirmation that validates the setup as a realistic possibility. The trigger can be news, additional research, computer signals, and chart patterns.	Action taken by the investor.

FIGURE 2.2

Seasonal Pattern in Walt Disney

Long	Enter: 12/14		Exit: 1/8		Stop %: 9	P/L Ratio: 6.1		Trade # 142865894
Entry Year	Date In	Price In	Date Out	Price Out		Profit/Loss	P/L Pct	Total P/L
1970	12/14	1.36	1/4	0.67		-0.69	-50.73	-0.69
1971	12/14	1.16	1/10	1.31		0.15	12.93	-0.54
1972	12/14	2.20	1/8	2.22		0.02	0.90	-0.52
1973	12/14	0.84	1/8	0.73		-0.11	-13.09	-0.63
1974	12/16	0.34	1/8	0.45		0.11	32.35	-0.52
1975	12/15	0.95	1/8	1.02		0.07	7.36	-0.45
1976	12/14	0.94	1/10	0.92		-0.02	-2.12	-0.47
1977	12/14	0.83	1/9	0.77		-0.06	-7.22	-0.53
1978	12/14	0.83	1/8	0.88		0.05	6.02	-0.48
1979	12/14	0.92	1/8	0.94		0.02	2.17	-0.46
1980	12/15	0.97	1/8	1.06		0.09	9.27	-0.37
1981	12/14	1.05	1/8	1.08		0.03	2.85	-0.34
1982	12/14	1.28	1/10	1.31		0.03	2.34	-0.31
1983	12/14	1.05	1/9	1.09		0.04	3.80	-0.27
1984	12/14	1.22	1/8	1.27		0.05	4.09	-0.22
1985	12/16	2.31	1/8	2.45		0.14	6.06	-0.08
1986	12/15	3.78	1/8	4.05		0.27	7.14	0.19
1987	12/14	4.80	1/8	4.86		0.06	1.25	0.25
1988	12/14	5.45	1/9	5.66		0.21	3.85	0.46
1989	12/14	10.89	12/20	9.31		-1.58	-14.50	-1.12
1990	12/14	8.56	1/8	7.94		-0.62	-7.24	-1.74
1991	12/16	9.08	1/8	10.19		1.11	12.22	-0.63
1992	12/14	13.48	1/8	14.36		0.88	6.52	0.25

FIGURE 2.2

Seasonal Pattern in Walt Disney, continued

Long Entry Year	Enter: 12/14 Date In	Price In	Exit: 1/8 Date Out	Stop %: 9 Price Out	P/L Ratio: 6.1 Profit/Loss	Trade # 142865894 P/L Pct	Total P/L
1993	12/16	13.98	1/10	15.91	1.93	13.80	2.18
1994	12/14	14.61	1/9	15.28	0.67	4.58	2.85
1995	12/14	20.23	1/8	20.66	0.43	2.12	3.28
1996	12/16	23.09	1/8	22.59	−0.50	−2.16	2.78
1997	12/15	32.34	1/8	32.53	0.19	0.58	2.97
1998	12/14	30.63	1/8	32.56	1.93	6.30	4.90
1999	12/14	28.50	1/10	35.88	7.38	25.89	12.28
2000	12/14	29.00	1/8	30.13	1.13	3.89	13.41
2001	12/14	20.97	1/8	22.79	1.82	8.67	15.23
2002	12/16	16.88	1/8	17.68	0.80	4.73	16.03
2003	12/15	22.83	1/8	24.96	2.13	9.32	18.16

Trades: 34	Winners: 27	Losers: 7	% Winners: 79.41	Daily PF: 0.0322
Avg Prof: 0.8051	Avg Loss: −0.5114	% Avg Prof: 7.44	% Avg Loss: −13.87	

There has been a strong tendency for the price of Walt Disney (DIS) stock to go up from approximately 14 December through about 8 January. In fact, this tendency has repeated itself about 79 percent of the time in the last 34 years. The first step in the STF method is to find historical patterns. In this case, we begin our plan with a highly reliable and repetitive pattern.

◤ **FIGURE 2.3** ▶ Historical Pattern with Timing Trigger in DIS

As you can see, this trade worked out perfectly, making yet another profit in 2003.

Now that I have shown you the GIM and STF and explained some of the details, there are a few more issues that need to be addressed. The following questions and issues are probably on your mind. Rest assured they will be answered. For now, I ask your patience and commitment.

- How can I begin with only a few hundred dollars?
- How can I get the money to begin investing, if I don't have it yet?

- How do I know if I'm trying to move ahead too quickly?
- How do I know if I'm moving too slowly?
- Should I try to have opinions, or just follow rules?
- Are opinions worthwhile, or just potentially problematic?
- Should I try to do this alone, or with a partner?
- What, if any, are the dangers of working alone?
- What, if any, are the dangers of working with a partner?
- Am I capable of going it alone, or am I more likely to be successful with a partner or partners?

As you read the chapters that follow, all of the above questions will be answered.

3

Financial "True Confessions"

Before you learn my trading methods, I encourage you to read this chapter because it will help you determine your "readiness" to be a stock trader. A few hours spent reading and studying this chapter will be an investment well worth your while. Consider the following questions.

How did you learn to invest? Did you read a book, a few books, many books? Did you attend a seminar, a workshop, or a night-school course? Did you take a seminar online? Did you learn from a friend?

Are you self-taught? No matter how you learned or who taught you, the fact is that if you're not making money in the market, it's due to one of three causes: what you learned doesn't work and probably never did; you may be using the system incorrectly; or you may even have a psychological problem that prevents you from implementing a system effectively. Let's look at these three possibilities in greater detail:

1. *Your method of investing or trading isn't making money because it doesn't work.* This is very common and not at all surprising. Most things you have learned or read about don't work. They are marginal at best, losing propositions at worst. But why? It would seem that with all the advances in computer technology and the ability to analyze stocks, there would be many good ways to make consistent money in the stock market. Yet in spite of these advances there are still many losers in the markets. The irony of this situation is that even the best money managers lose money when markets decline! What's even more interesting is that not all money managers can achieve good results, even in markets that are going up. Why would that be the case? The simple truth is that there are very few good methods or systems for making money in the stock market. If the method you have been using doesn't work, at least there is one consolation: you're not alone. Misery loves company. One of the major goals of this book is to help you change your losing ways.

2. *What if you know that your method of trading stocks works for others but it's not working for you?* Yes, that DOES happen much more frequently than you may think. But how does something like that happen? Your uncle Louie told you about a system he's been using for stocks. He showed you the results and you were impressed. He even taught you how to use it. He's making money but you're not. What's

even worse is that you told several friends about the method and they're making money but you're not. What's the problem? How could this be? What a shame. How embarrassing! What has gone wrong? There are several possibilities, such as:

a. You didn't learn the method correctly

b. You are not applying the method correctly, or

c. You're making mistakes due to poor discipline and/or investor psychology.

3. *Item c addresses the behavioral and psychological or emotional aspects of investing.* Believe it or not, this is often the biggest cause for losses in the financial markets. Poor investor psychology and faulty discipline account for a good percentage of losses. The best trading or investment methods are utterly useless in the hands of an undisciplined or overly emotional investor. In my more than 35 years of experience in the equity and futures markets, I have seen more traders lose money due to poor psychology and poor trade-selection methods. This is SO IMPORTANT that I will devote several chapters to solving problems caused by trader psychology. The bottom line here is that you can't kick ass if you're getting your ass kicked!

▶ Play a Little Game

In order to become a successful investor you need to level with yourself and admit to your shortcomings. You also have to give yourself praise for your strong points. Let's cut through your defensive layers and be direct and honest for a change. You can tell your friends or lovers anything you want to about your prowess as an investor, but *entre nous* (between you and me), take a few minutes to strip away the years of BS and look in the mirror. If this exercise offends you then I respectfully submit that you are either so very successful that you don't need this book, or you're so defensive that you need to see a good shrink before you sink another penny into the sewer hole of your investing losses. If you don't want to fess up to your problems, I suggest that you return this book immediately.

Here is a checklist that I'd like you to complete before you move on to the next chapter. By the time you finish reading with the next chapter, you will have answers to the following important questions:

- Am I losing money because I don't have a good trading system or method?
- Am I losing money because I am not emotionally suited to be an investor?
- Is there hope for me?
- Where am I going wrong in my investments and trading?
- What are the tools I need in order to keep my ass from getting kicked?
- Do I have problems on several different levels?
- Are my problems simple or difficult to cure?
- What steps can I take to change my losing ways and become a winning investor?

Testing Yourself

I assume that because you've gotten this far you are willing to take the next step. Before you do, however, I ask you to be brutally honest in your replies. Remember that this little assessment is designed to help you. Frankly, it makes no difference to me if you're dishonest with yourself. If, however, you plan to be dishonest, don't even waste your time reading the items on my list. I'll be completely blunt with you: if you want to BS yourself then you'll get BS results; you'll have reached BS conclusions and you'll continue to be grist for the mill of professional investors and traders. I suppose that in a way that's good. You'll have fulfilled an economic purpose by contributing your money to the pool of available winnings. OK, I've "hammered" you enough. Let's get on with my list of questions. I suggest that you make a copy of these pages and underline or circle your replies.

PLEASE ANSWER THESE QUESTIONS AS **TRUE** OR **FALSE**.

1. I make my investment and trading decisions based on a variety of factors. I evaluate these factors and then I make a "gut feeling" decision about buying, selling, or holding a stock. ❑ TRUE ❑ FALSE

2. I have a very specific trading approach that uses totally objective rules for entry and exit, but I am still losing money in the market in spite of the fact that my system has been back tested with excellent results. ❑ TRUE ❑ FALSE

3. I know the rules I need to follow but I consistently ignore them. ❑ TRUE ❑ FALSE

4. I have never been able to follow a specific set of trading rules effectively. ❑ TRUE ❑ FALSE

5. I tend to get out of my winning trades quickly, but I hold on to my losers until they grow hair on them. ❑ TRUE ❑ FALSE

6. I am easily influenced by the news, by my broker, and by stock tips. When this happens I lose my discipline and make bad trading decisions. ❑ TRUE ❑ FALSE

7. I get my best stock tips and advice by visiting internet chat rooms. ❑ TRUE ❑ FALSE

8. I have been trading and investing for more than two years without profitable results. ❑ TRUE ❑ FALSE

9. My losing trades are most often larger than my winning trades. ❑ TRUE ❑ FALSE

10. I have been successful in my business or profession, but I can't seem to be successful as an investor no matter what I do. ❑ TRUE ❑ FALSE

.06 +1.3	BL	InTE	9.69	+.04 +2.1	IM	FF2010n	13.12	-.07 +1.4	BL	FndofAmY	25.20	-.14 +5.0	MC	
.03 +2.5	IL	Mgdln	9.35	+.02 +4.0	AB	FF2020n	13.07	-.11 +1.0	XC	GlobalA	35.41	+.07 +6.3	GL	SmlCapGr
.09 +.9	BL	STGvSec	7.11	+1.1	SU	FF2030n	12.99	-.14 +.5	XC	OverseasA	19.59	+.04 +7.8	IL	SmallCo
										SoGenGold n15.85		+.55 -9.0	AU	USGovSec

Evaluating the Results

Now that you've taken my little "quiz" (and I hope you've been honest), let's examine your replies in detail. This process will help you achieve the following results:

- You will get an idea of where you stand as an investor.
- You will know your weaknesses and strengths.
- You will know how much work you have ahead of you.
- You will get a clear idea of how to overcome your behavioral and/or psychological challenges.

This will prepare you for the strategies I will teach you later on. While this is not a definitive test of your skills or readiness to trade, I believe it will give you a good idea of where you stand. While there are not purely right or wrong answers, there are answers that correlate highly with success and others that are heavily related to failure. Here is how to evaluate your results:

1. I make my investment and trading decisions based on a variety of factors. I evaluate these factors and then I make a "gut feeling" decision about buying, selling or holding a stock. ❏ TRUE ❏ FALSE

   Answer. If you answered TRUE then give yourself a –1 (minus 1). If you make any decision based on "gut feeling" then your odds of success are not good. All hope is not lost, though, because you have the potential to be successful. You simply need more education.

2. I have a very specific trading approach that uses totally objective rules for entry and exit, but I am still losing money in the market in spite of the fact that my system has been back-tested with excellent results. ❏ TRUE ❏ FALSE

   Answer. If you answered TRUE, then give yourself a –1. If you are following a good system and are still losing money, then you likely have discipline problems and must overcome them if you are to be a winner. The good news is that you have a method. All you need now is to learn how to use it consistently.

3. I know the rules I need to follow but I consistently ignore them. ❏ TRUE ❏ FALSE

   Answer. If you answered TRUE, then give yourself a –1. If you know the rules and don't follow them, you have a problem you need to overcome if you are to be successful. The good news, however, is that you know the rules. So there is hope for you!

4. I have never been able to follow a specific set of trading rules effectively. ❏ TRUE ❏ FALSE

   Answer. If you answered TRUE, then give yourself a –1. The reason should be obvious.

5. I tend to get out of my winning trades quickly, but I hold on to my losers until they grow hair on them.
   ❏ TRUE ❏ FALSE

   Answer. If you answered TRUE, then give yourself a –1. The reason should be obvious.

6. I am easily influenced by the news, by my broker, and by stock tips. When this happens, I lose my discipline and make bad trading decisions. ❏ TRUE ❏ FALSE

   Answer. If you answered TRUE, then give yourself a –1. If you lose your discipline, you lose everything. This one is a big "no-no." You have a long way to go before you allow yourself to put another penny into the market.

7. I get my best stock tips and advice by visiting internet chat rooms. ❏ TRUE ❏ FALSE

   Answer. If you answered TRUE, then give yourself a –1. Most people who visit stock chat rooms are either insecure, uninformed, losers in the stock market, or promoters who seek to promote their stocks to an unsuspecting group of suckers. If you're an investment chat room addict, do yourself a favor and stay away!

8. I have been trading and investing for more than two years without profitable results. ❏ TRUE ❏ FALSE

.05 +1.3	BL	IntTE	9.69	+.04 +2.1	IM	FF2010n	13.12	-.07 +1.4	BL	FndofAmY	25.20	-.14 +5.0	MC	MgSec
.03 +2.5	IL	Mgdln	9.35	+.02 +4.0	AB	FF2020n	13.07	-.11 +1.0	XC	GlobalA	35.41	+.07 +6.3	GL	SmiCapGr
.08 +.9	BL	STGvSec	7.11	+1.1	SU	FF2030n	12.99	-.14 +.5	XC	OverseasA	19.59	+.04 +7.8	IL	SmallCo
.10 +.3	XC									SoGenGold n15.85		+.55 -9.0	ALI	USGovSec

Answer. If you answered TRUE, then give yourself a –1. If you have indeed been trading for more than two years with losing results, it means you've been doing something dreadfully wrong and you need to make some big changes before you invest another penny!

9. My losing trades are most often larger than my winning trades. ❑ TRUE ❑ FALSE

Answer. If you answered TRUE, then give yourself a –1. Your winning trades obviously need to be larger than your losing trades if you plan to make money at this game.

10. I have been successful in my business or profession but I can't seem to be successful as an investor no matter what I do. ❑ TRUE ❑ FALSE

Answer. If you answered TRUE, then give yourself a –1. But all hope is not lost. Since you have a record of success then there is a good chance that you will be successful as a trader but you're not ready to trade as yet. You need more education

EVALUATE YOURSELF

Now that you have your score, take a look at the cold hard facts.

- If you have no minus scores, you are ready to trade, or you're already making money.
- If you have two minus scores, then you have good odds for success by honing your skills using the methods in this book.
- If you scored four minuses or more, you need to take your time and learn the methods in this book. You must also learn to apply them with strict discipline if you plan to succeed.

Do yourself a favor and be honest in your self-evaluation. If you want to fritter your money away and be grist for the mill of professional traders, then keep doing what you're doing. But if you sincerely want to be successful, you'll take heed and learn your lessons well.

▶ A Universal Eternal Truth

The bottom line to all the above verbiage is simple. What I am about to tell you is the universal truth of investing and trading. The ultimate and underlying reality of all that's contained in this book, and in the thousands of other books written about investing, is that no matter what strategy, method, system, computer program, technique, or methodology you use in the markets, none of them will make you money consistently UNLESS YOU ARE ABLE to use them with discipline, objectivity, and lack of emotion. That's it! That's the bottom line. That's the major defining factor.

Let me make it even less complicated. The best investment advice is totally worthless in the hands of an individual who cannot, for various and sundry reasons, employ it. In my work as a market analyst, researcher, and trader, I have seen literally thousands of traders and investors engage in literally hundreds of losing behaviors.

4

Technical versus Fundamental Trading

There are many different ways to make money (and lose money) in the stock market. There are more ways to lose money than there are ways of making money. Most investors are very familiar with ways to lose money. New ways to lose money are being discovered every day. In my more than 35 years of experience in securities and commodities trading I have seen practically every losing way, and I have even done my share to come up with some new ones. Those days are over for me. I hope that this book will help those days be over for you as well.

The two broad categories of trading and investing are based on two radically different methodologies. The vast majority of investors, market analysts, and money managers make their decisions based on an approach called fundamental analysis (FA). Although FA is the most commonly used method for making investment and trading decisions, it is not necessarily the best. While the defenders of FA will vehemently defend their methods, their position is not fully defensible given the facts. Before I dig into this controversy, I'll give you a working definition of FA.

Fundamental analysis is a method of making investing and/or trading decisions that considers the economic facts of a stock. These facts include such things as earnings, corporate management, inventories, costs, the general economic trend, legal issues, competition, the product or products being sold, pending orders, taxes, and pending new products.

Those who make decisions based on FA believe that these factors ultimately determine the price at which a stock will sell. They spend a considerable amount of time gathering their facts and figures. They examine their fundamentals in terms of the current price, and project where prices might go as a function of the fundamentals. They then make their decisions to buy, sell, or hold based on their analyses.

Is the FA method worthwhile? If you ask those who practice FA they will, of course, support their method. They will tell you that FA not only makes sense, but that it makes money as well. They will tell you that the ultimate fundamentals are the only consistent determinant of prices. But are they right? Here are some things to consider when it comes to using FA as your method of selecting stocks:

- By the time fundamentals are known, they may very well be out-of-date and no longer applicable.
- Are the fundamentals you have collected really important?

- How can you obtain the necessary information?
- Are your sources credible?
- Are the fundamentals you have gathered correct? As an example, consider the case of Enron. The company continued to report stellar earnings while their books were being "cooked" and false earnings were being reported. Even the most savvy investors and money managers were completely fooled by the Enron deception.
- Why do stocks with very good fundamentals still decline?
- Even if the fundamentals are known, how do you know exactly when to buy and when to sell?
- Does knowledge of the fundamentals tell you when you are wrong? By this I mean, do the fundamentals tell you how much to risk?

These are some of the major issues confronting those who use FA in their analyses. As you can see, the task is not only significant but also requires a level of expertise that not all investors have. As a result, professionals who understand and use FA have developed a public following. Since most investors are not able to perform the necessary analyses, they turn the task over to professionals. This suits professionals quite well because they have a captive client who depends on them for advice and decisions. Professional money managers make good money on management fees and other profits.

The task of FA is intimidating to most investors. Not only are they unaware of the methods but they are also overwhelmed by the task. Their insecurity discourages them from investing on their own. They have, over the years, been misled to believe that professional money managers are nothing less than demigods, given their expertise in stock-picking. There are a few (very few) professional money managers who are truly good at their jobs. I'm certain that my comments will anger many professionals, but I can only say what I believe to be true based on my own experiences.

The sad fact is that most money managers can only make money when stocks are rising. When stocks decline, they lose money (and all too often lots of it). Money managers who run hedge funds (funds that buy stocks and sell them short) tend to do much better, but investing with them is much more risky.

If FA were all it is claimed to be, money managers and investors who use this as their method of stock selection would be skilled enough to buy stocks before they move up, and to be entirely out of stocks before they decline. But sadly, this is not the case. Figures 4.1 through 4.3 show the performance of several top mutual funds during the period just prior to and after the 2000 stock market top. As you can see, all the mutual funds noted lost money while the stock market was declining. Why would managers of these funds be recommending them if they had the knowledge they needed from their use of FA?

In light of these undeniable facts, I respectfully submit that FA, even if used properly, does not provide investors or traders with sufficient valuable information to make money consistently. But is there a viable alternative? I urge you to consider the other major approach, technical analysis (TA).

▶ Technical Analysis

The technical approach to market analysis is infinitely more sensible to me. I am certain that my strong support of this approach will ruffle many feathers in the investment community, but this does not concern me. My one and only goal is to give you your best shot at making money based on my 35 years of experience in the markets. Given this vast experience, I am firmly convinced that the lessons I have learned can be of considerable value to you.

What Is TA?

I will spend more time on the TA method than on the FA method simply because I believe that TA is a far better approach for more nonprofessional investors. Simply explained, TA is a method of analyzing markets that does not require any attention to fundamentals. It is, as its name suggests, technical. By technical, I mean that the approach looks at a variety of factors that are a function of stock prices and related statistical data, as opposed to the underlying causes of market movements. The technical approach to stock market analysis looks at the following factors, either individually or in combination:

- Price and price trends
- Charts and graphs of price movements
- Mathematical derivations of prices, such as moving averages, oscillators, and other indicators
- Trading volume
- Price patterns
- Cyclical factors
- Seasonal patterns and relationships
- Chart patterns
- Support and resistance patterns
- Intermarket relationships
- Market-sentiment indicators
- Artificial-intelligence methods, and
- Variations on the themes of these factors

There are literally hundreds if not, in fact, thousands of methods that fall under the TA rubric. Given the multiplicity of methods, it behooves us to find and settle upon those that are most closely correlated with profits. But this can be an arduous task.

Some traditional proponents of FA consider TA to be a voodoo approach to stock analysis. They do not believe that TA can lead investors to make profitable decisions. Yet the professional technical analyst would argue that the ultimate indicator of a stock's value is price. They (and I) claim that if you can ascertain the probable direction of price by examining the various determinants of price, you can be a winning investor.

Don't get me wrong. I'm not saying that FA is no good. I'm not saying that FA can't make you money. And I'm not saying that FA is a waste of time. What I'm saying is that TA is faster, easier to learn, less expensive to apply, logical, sensible, more immediate, and, above all, a valid indication or predictor of future price movements. Of course, the degree to which you will be successful with TA is a function of your skill and discipline. No matter how good a method of stock analysis may be, it is useless in the hands of a foolish or undisciplined investor.

Many Methods and Opinions

As in the case of virtually all methods and approaches to analyzing markets, there are many choices. The sad but true fact is that the great majority of TA methods are essentially useless, either because they do not work or because they are not sufficiently objective. One of the goals I have set for this book is to give you TA methods that are objective and effective. In every case I will attempt to provide you with historical and/or statistical validation for the methods so that you will be confident in using them. One of the most important things I have learned in my many years of trading and investing is that if investors lack confidence in what they are doing, the result will be negative, because they will not follow through consistently or correctly in the prescribed approach.

▶ The Essence of Technical Analysis

Without a doubt, the profitable use of TA is dependent upon the following:
- Rules must be 100 percent objective.
- Because TA gives you buy, hold, and/or sell signals, these indicators must be specific and not subject to any interpretation. All situations are either white or black. Either you are a

buyer or a seller. If you are not a buyer or a seller, then you have no position.

- The method must not only tell you when to buy or sell, but must also give you a specific place to exit your stock(s) if you are wrong. No method or technique in the stock market or, for that matter, in any form of investing, is 100 percent correct.
- The method should give you an idea of how much money you can make. Although this information is not vital, it is helpful.
- The method should also tell you which stock or stocks to buy or sell. There are thousands of stocks. Because you cannot invest in all of them, you must be selective. Picking and choosing randomly or on the basis of gut feelings will not work for you. You need a specific and consistent approach.
- You need to be consistent in your application of the rules.
- You need to do your "homework" by studying stocks at regular intervals as prescribed by the system or method you are using.
- You need to practice solid risk management principles in order to maximize profits and minimize losses.

Indeed, there are more rules and procedures, but these are the most important ones to follow. As I explain the other methods, I will familiarize you with the details. But do not assume that they are any less important. You must always think of investing and trading as a business. If you follow the rules and do your job with patience, persistence, and consistency, you will have consistent success. If, however, you apply the methods I will teach you without consistency, you will become a statistic as you join the ranks of losers.

Examples of TA

Now let's take a look at a few examples of TA as it is used in the stock selection process.

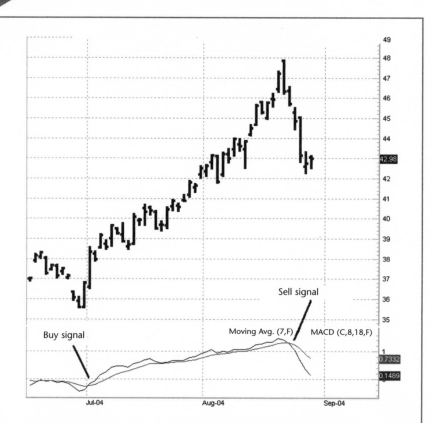

FIGURE 4.1 MACD Technical Timing Trigger

This chart shows the MACD technical timing indicator as it triggers a buy and then a sell signal.

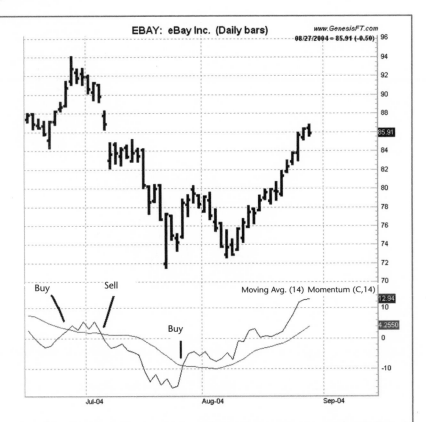

FIGURE 4.2 Momentum and Moving Average Technical Method

This chart shows the use of momentum and a moving average as another technical method for buying and selling stocks. A buy signal occurs when momentum moves above its moving average. A sell signal occurs when momentum falls below its moving average.

FIGURE 4.3 ▶ Moving Average Channel Technical Method

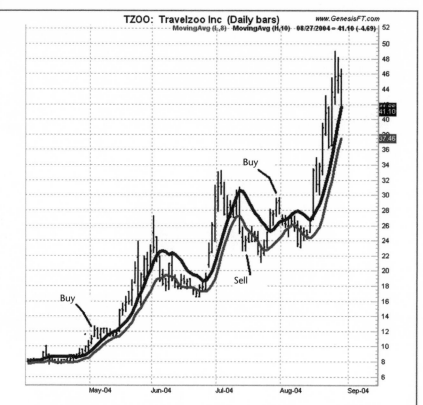

The Moving Average Channel technical method for stock timing, showing buy and sell signals.

CHAPTER

5

A Closer Look
at Technical Analysis
Concepts

Many investors and traders have been attracted to the use of technical analysis since the early 1970s. Yet in spite of the voluminous material available on this topic, there are still many who are uncertain about the difference between a timing indicator, a trading system, a trading method, and a trading technique. As you have likely concluded by now, the concepts and methods discussed in this book are primarily based on technical analysis concepts. The following definitions and overviews will help you understand these terms as they are used in this book and by technical traders in the financial markets. Although only a few of these concepts and methods will be described in this book, they are, nonetheless, worth learning if you plan to be a technical trader.

▶ Market Timing and Timing Indicators

The term "market timing" has, since the late 1990s become somewhat of a "dirty word" in the financial markets. The implication that market timing is either unethical or illegal owes its origin to the fact that a number of mutual fund managers and/or their employees acted illegally in trading their own shares in the fund for short-term swings, using timing methods to take advantage of price anomalies in their shares and the actual value of their shares. This has given market timing a bad name. As usual, those who jump to conclusions are either uninformed or misinformed. In actuality, marketing is not only a positive approach to trading—it can also be highly profitable. And as long as traders do not violate existing securities laws, it is perfectly legal. Not all traders, however, have the skills, knowledge, or discipline to make a profit as market timers. Carefully applied, the tools in this book will elevate you to the level of a successful market timer.

▶ What Is a Timing Indicator?

A *timing indicator* (also known as a timing signal) helps traders determine the optimum time and/or price at which to enter a given stock. Investors use timing signals and timing indicators as a tool to help them determine when a stock should be bought or sold. The accuracy or effectiveness of a timing signal is increased if it is based on a valid concept or theory of market behavior. If your timing signals are based on arbitrary ideas, they will be less effective than if they were based on actual, verifiable characteristics of market behavior. There are literally thousands of ideas upon which timing indicators and signals are based. Some are valid, while others are either mythical or mystical, with no historical validity. They are, therefore, useless.

Traders and investors use timing indicators and timing signals to increase their probability of success in the stock market. All too often traders use timing indicators that are essentially ineffective. Unfortunately, many popular timing indicators are about as accurate as a coin toss. Most of the timing indicators in popular use today yield results that are only slightly better than what might be achieved by throwing darts. The average investor is unaware of this, because most popular books sing the praises of their favorite timing indicators without providing any statistics as to how well these indicators or signals perform. I have done everything possible to provide you with statistical validation for the methods discussed in this book.

Timing indicators are very useful tools in short-term stock trading. They can perform even better when used as part of a trading system or method. Trading systems and methods are discussed later in this chapter. In summary, then, timing signals and indicators are technically based configurations that provide us with setups for possible trades (remember our STF method?). They are not calls to action (i.e., triggers). Examples of several timing indicators, their assets and liabilities, are discussed later in this chapter.

TRADING SYSTEMS

A *trading system* is a complete approach to buying and selling stocks (or futures) that is totally systematic. It contains all the major elements of the STF method. It is based on concise and specific rules that are operationally defined, and capable of being implemented by anyone who is familiar with the system rule and procedures. A trading system contains rules for market entry, market exit, and risk management. As I am sure you will recall, these are the three major elements of the STF method. An excellent resource

.05 +1.3	BL	IntTE	9.69	+.04 +2.1	IM	FF2010n	13.12	−.07 +1.4	BL	FndofAmY	25.20	−.14 +5.0	MC	MidSel s
.03 +2.5	IL	Mgdln	9.35	+.02 +4.0	AB	FF2020n	13.07	−.11 +1.0	XC	GlobalA	35.41	+.07 +6.3	GL	SmlCapGr
.09 +.9	BL	STGvSec	7.11	+1.1	SU	FF2030n	12.99	−.14 +.5	XC	OverseasA	19.59	+.04 +7.8	IL	SmallCo
.10 +.3	XC									SoGenGold n15.85		+.55 −9.0	ALL	USGovSec

for more information on trading systems is the Perry Kaufman book *Commodity Trading Systems and Methods* (Wiley and Sons).

The rules of a trading system ideally allow the trader to reproduce historical performance of the system as long as the system was developed correctly to produce results that can be replicated in real time. By this I mean that the mere development and back-testing of a trading system do not assure us that the system will move forward in real time with similar results. If developed correctly, however, trading systems should yield essentially the same results regardless of the trader. The most appealing feature of a trading system is that many traders can make exactly the same decisions because they are using the same system. If the rules of the system are completely objective, and if the traders using the system are disciplined in applying the rules, their end results (i.e., profits or losses) should be about the same.

Some investors complain that trading systems are too rigid, too disciplined, or that they do not allow individuals to apply their own valid experience when making market decisions. In my experience, few investors have sufficient experience or knowledge that can be of benefit. And even if they do, they rarely apply that knowledge consistently.

Newcomers to the trading arena are urged to use a systematic approach to trading because it will force them to be disciplined. This will increase their odds of making money. The benefits of sticking to the rules of a profitable trading system are obvious. Yet another benefit of using a trading system is that if and when you HAVE lost money, a review of the rules allows you to readily pinpoint where the system has failed, or if it is you who has failed. When you stray from your system, identifying your mistakes becomes more difficult.

TRADING METHODS

A trading method is a combination of timing signals loosely organized and implemented according to a variety of relatively general

5	+1.3	BL		IntTE	9.69	+.04 +2.1	IM		FF2010n	13.12	-.07 +1.4	BL		FndotAmY	25.20	-.14 +5.0	MC		MidSecS	1
3	+2.5	IL		Mgdln	9.35	+.02 +4.0	AB		FF2020n	13.07	-.11 +1.0	XC		GlobalA	35.41	+.07 +6.3	GL		SmlCapGro	1
9	+.9	BL		STGvSec	7.11	+1.1	SU		FF2030n	12.99	-.14 +.5	XC		OverseasA	19.59	+.04 +7.8	IL		SmnllCo	1
0	+.3	XC												SoGenGold	n15.85	+.55 -9.0	AU		USuovSecs	1

rules. Trading methods fall just short of trading systems in their degree of completeness. Most traders who believe they are using a trading system are actually using a trading method. The investor determines when to buy and sell based on his or her rules, yet these rules are often neither highly specific, nor are they sufficiently thorough. Furthermore, the follow-through aspect of the approach is often lacking in specificity.

Using a trading method instead of a trading system often means that a certain amount of subjectivity will enter into the decision-making process. Depending on whether you see subjectivity as an asset or a liability in trading, you will find the use of a trading method either profitable or unacceptable. In recent years, trading methods have come to be known as "proprietary trading." In using this approach, the trader uses a trading *method* (as opposed to a trading *system*) to make decisions. I strongly advise you to use a trading system as opposed to a trading method. The degree of subjectivity that trading methods allow is an open invitation to losses for beginning investors.

▶ Types of Timing Indicators

There are three main categories of timing indicators in general use today. They are as follows:

1. LEADING INDICATORS

These are indicators that give you buy or sell signals before a stock changes its direction.

Leading indicators are the most useful and effective indicators because they allow ample time for you to prepare to make your trade(s). When applying leading indicators to stocks, remember this: The indicator tells you that a move is likely to happen. This is the setup portion of the STF method. Although it would appear that leading indicators offer the investor the best of all possible worlds, there are drawbacks when using such indicators. One major problem occurs because it is easy to buy a stock too early. Exposure to price fluctuations that occur before the beginning of the indicated up or down trend may cause you to exit early. If you are willing to take a certain amount of risk only in a particular investment, and have bought early because you are using a leading indicator, you may be stopped out of your trade, and thus lose all potential for profit. This is why you MUST ALWAYS REMEMBER to use a trigger with your leading indicator setup. Several of the methods described in this book are leading indicators. When used with their appropriate follow-through methods, they become trading systems.

2. TIME-CURRENT INDICATORS

These indicators tend to turn higher or lower at about the same time that a stock does.

There are many such indicators. Some of them are discussed later in this chapter. They can be very helpful in making long-term investments, and we consider such indicators just about as useful as leading indicators. The time-current indicator should not expose you to as many of the pre-move price fluctuations as the leading indicator does. When using a time-current indicator, your decisions about buying and selling must be made quickly inasmuch as the stock should be making its move at the same time that you take your position. If you tarry, you may be too late.

3. LAGGING INDICATORS

True to their name, these indicators lag behind stock moves.

Such indicators are, by their very nature, late to indicate a change in the direction of a stock. The stock moves first, and the lagging indicator moves after it. These indicators are also known as *trend-following indicators* because they follow trends but do not attempt to forecast them. Using lagging indicators to make decisions about buying and selling tends to be inaccurate because you are always buying or selling AFTER a change in the trend has developed.

The use of lagging indicators for long-term decisions is an effective and acceptable method of investing if you are willing and able to sit through market moves against you. At times these moves can be lengthy and substantial in size. If, however, you are positioning yourself for market moves that may take a year or more to develop, lagging indicators can help you be confident that you have bought or sold after a true change in the trend.

Remember that lagging indicators tend to be somewhat inaccurate. By this I mean you may very well be buying at tops and getting out at bottoms too often—clearly a losing strategy. Hence, lagging indicators must be chosen carefully as a function of their characteristics, or they must be used in conjunction with other indicators that will minimize their inherent lack of accuracy. The goal in using a lagging indicator is that the trader or investor will be able to profitably capture a significant portion of a trend before the indicator changes direction again. In strong bull or bear markets, leading indicators do excellent work; however, in sideways markets or markets in transition, they tend to lose money due to their low accuracy.

Price versus Time: The Quintessential Consideration

While many traders and investors are good at discerning the trend of a market, their timing is often poor. Although such people may be able to tell you that a stock will move in a given direction, they themselves often have a hard time profiting from their knowledge because their market entries and exits are timed incorrectly. They may buy too late or too early, or they may sell too late or too early. This is very likely due to a lack of experience in using timing when getting into and out of trades.

Price is the single most important consideration to the long-term investor. Timing is the most important consideration to the short-term trader. Effective timing can overcome the importance of price. Investors and traders must take their actions with the existing trend rather than against it. In other words, the path of least resistance is to trade with the trend. One of the most important trend rules you will learn is that declining prices tend to continue their declines while rising prices tend to continue their climb (up to a point).

Expert opinions vary markedly with regard to the importance of price vs. timing. Odds are that an investment and/or trading approach that combines both elements is likely to be more productive and profitable in the long run than a one-sided method. The confluence of time and price is very important. The investor who can understand and use both price and time effectively is likely to enjoy consistent profits.

The concept of time and price confluence, when used as a trading system, is a significant and effective approach to making money. While the concept is valid, putting it into practice is a different issue entirely. Numerous systems and methods have been developed for the sole purpose of putting this concept into practice.

Someone who buys at support as prices decline in an existing uptrend is attempting to harness the power of this approach. The same is true when one sells short at resistance. In other words, the investor is attempting to combine price with time by selling at a given price after seeing the market rally, or buying at support when a market declines. Being able to discern the trend and the price at which to take a position is a powerful skill that should be mastered, or at least understood, by even the smallest investor.

In order to know exactly when to buy and sell, you will need to be able to define the following variables:

- *Trend.* What is the current trend? Is the trend up, down, or sideways? How "strong" is the trend? Is there a way to quantify the trend? What is the "quality" of the trend? Is the market moving sharply higher with considerable rapidity and magnitude, or is the trend slow and steady?

- *Support.* If the trend is up, is there a way to determine where a stock should stop its decline when it goes down (temporarily) during a pervasive uptrend? Can a specific price be determined and, if so, how?

- *Resistance.* If the trend is down, is there a way to determine where a stock should stop its rally when it goes up (temporarily) during a pervasive downtrend? Can a specific price be determined and, if so, how?

The fact is that all three can be ascertained with relative ease. For the time being, suffice it to say that specific methods for doing so will be presented. Our intent at this juncture is simply to introduce you to the concept. Here, then, are some methods for determining trends and/or entry/exit points. In each case, we will explain the method as well as its assets, liabilities, and variations. An example of each technique will be provided in chart form. If you are a newcomer to the markets, this synopsis will be very valuable to you whether you follow the methods taught in this book or not.

▶ Basic Timing Indicators

Given the plethora of trading systems, timing indicators, and methods available to the trader, it is reasonable to expect that most readers will be overwhelmed by the number of choices. Often the amount of available information in texts or online is insufficient to help you make a decision. In the long run, you are left to make decisions on your own. And, all too often, these decisions cannot be made without reference to historical performance. As you can imagine, this poses a formidable challenge to the newcomer. But this is no surprise. Information about what works or what doesn't work in the markets is often not available to the public in spite of all the books, seminars, and courses that are available.

The explanations that follow will help clarify the indicators and methods that we feel work best, and under what circumstances. I

.05	+1.3	BL		IntTE	9.69	+.04	+2.1	IM		FF2010n	13.12	-.07	+1.4	BL		FndofAmY	25.20	-.14	+5.0	MC		MigSec
.03	+2.5	IL		MgdIn	9.35	+.02	+4.0	AB		FF2020n	13.07	-.11	+1.0	XC		GlobalA	35.41	+.07	+6.3	GL		SmiCapGr
.09	+.9	BL		STGvSec	7.11		+1.1	SU		FF2000n	12.99	-.14	+.5	XC		OverseasA	19.59	+.04	+7.8	IL		SmallCo
.10	+.3	XC														SoGenGold n 15.85		+.55	-9.0	AU		USGovSec

will give you an evaluation of their assets and liabilities, all based on my considerable experience in the stock and commodity markets.

Moving Average Indicators (MAs): Traditional and Advanced

Whether you use one, two, or many MAs, the concepts and applications are essentially similar. Either the market price must close above or below its MAs to signal a buy or a sell, or the MAs themselves must change their relationship to one another in order to signal a trade. Richard Donchian popularized this approach in the 1950s, although it was probably being used well before then.

In the typical MA-based system, signals are generated in any of several ways:

- Price closes above or below its MA. Closing above the MA is considered a buy signal, whereas closing below the MA is considered a sell signal.
- In the case of multiple MAs, the approach signals buy or sell signals when the various lengths of MAs cross one another.
- In the case of MAs of closing/opening, or high or low prices, signals are generated when crossovers of the MAs occur as defined by the theory or method.

STRENGTHS

Traditional MA indicators tend to do extremely well in major trends. They can make you a lot of money after a major trend has started if you are able to hold on to your position. MAs are lagging indicators because they give signals *after* a market has made its turn. There are numerous variations on the theme of the MA—some more effective and responsive than others. Most computer trading systems allow you to use different mathematical formulations of the MA (that is, weighted, exponential, smoothed, displaced, centered, and so on).

WEAKNESSES

These indicators tend to give many false (that is, losing) signals. They will often get you into a move well after it has started, and when a change in trend occurs, they will often get you out after you have given back a considerable amount of your profit. Such moving averages tend to be inaccurate, and often have considerable drawdown as well as numerous consecutive losing trades.

Variations on the Theme of Moving Averages

There are many variations on the theme of moving averages. These include MA-based oscillators such as the MACD, the MA Channel, and various high and/or low MA combinations.

STRENGTHS

These variations on the MA tend to be more accurate and more sensitive than simple MA combinations of the closing price. The MACD was specifically designed for S&P trading by Gerald Appel, while the Moving Average Channel (MAC) is "my creation."

WEAKNESSES

There is a tendency, as with many MA-based systems, to give back too much profit once a change in trend has developed. This is true of all lagging indicators.

Examples of Moving Average Signals are shown in Figures 5.1 and 5.2

Stochastics (SI) and the Relative Strength Index (RSI)

Dr. George Lane popularized the Stochastic Indicator (SI) and its use. The Relative Strength Index (RSI) is very similar to the SI. The difference is that SI has two values; RSI has only one. Computing a

FIGURE 5.1 Moving Average Buy and Sell Signals

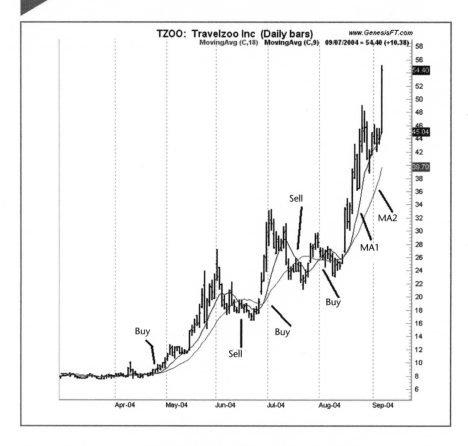

moving average of the first SI value yields the second SI value. Both indicators are often used to identify theoretically "overbought" or "oversold" conditions. They may both be used as timing indicators as well as indicators of so-called overbought and oversold conditions.

STRENGTHS

Both the RSI and SI have considerable sex appeal. By this we mean they look good on a chart. They tend to identify tops and bottoms

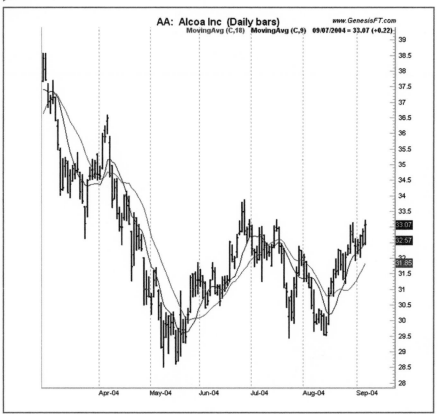

FIGURE 5.2 ▶ Dual Moving Average Indicator

quite well. They are also useful in timing, provided one uses the appropriate crossover areas for timing trades.

WEAKNESSES

The concepts of "overbought" and "oversold" are not useful and often misleading. Frequently markets that are overbought continue to go considerably higher, while markets that are oversold continue to go considerably lower.

Chart Patterns and Formations

These methods are based on the traditional techniques proposed by Edwards and Magee, as well as other tools such as those developed by W. D. Gann, George Bayer, and R. N. Elliott. There are many different chart formations and various outcomes possible for each. They require a good deal of study and are, at times, quite intricate as well as subjective. The trading literature is rich in methods and systems based on these patterns.

For examples see Figures 5.3 and 5.4.

FIGURE 5.3 The Scholastic Indicator Buy and Sell Signals

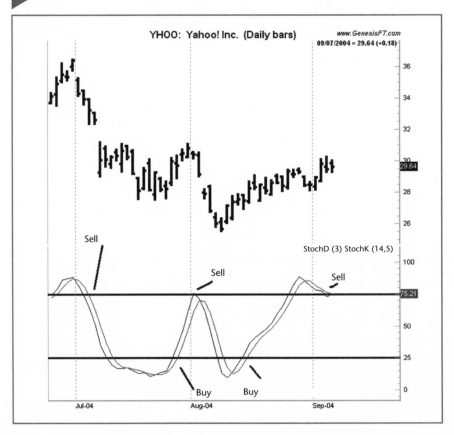

FIGURE 5.4 ▶ Scholastic Buy and Sell Signals

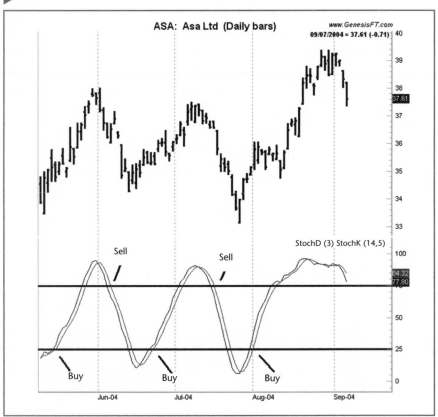

STRENGTHS

- *These methods are highly visual.* In other words, you can draw lines on a piece of paper, or you can examine patterns visually, to see what should be done.
- *The methods don't necessarily require a computer.*
- *They can easily be learned by almost anyone.* Frequently, the prescribed actions are specific once you have completed the necessary interpretation of the chart patterns.
- *The methods are usually quite logical.* Hence, they have a good deal of face validity.

WEAKNESSES

- In most cases these methods are highly subjective and difficult to test for accuracy.
- The Gann and Elliott methods have been known and used by traders for many years; however, there is considerable disagreement, even among experts, as to what patterns exist at any given point in time and, in fact, how these patterns should be traded.

Parabolic

This is a method that is based on a mathematical formula derived from the parabolic curve. It provides the trader with two values each day, a "sell number" and a "buy number." These serve as sell stops and buy stops. Penetration of the buy number means to go long and close out short, while penetration of the sell number means to close out long and go short.

STRENGTHS

- The parabolic indicator is totally objective. It can be used as a mechanical trading system with risk management methods.
- It provides a buy and sell stop daily and is therefore capable of changing orientation from long to short very quickly.

WEAKNESSES

- Parabolic can get "whipsawed" badly in sideways or highly volatile markets.
- Parabolic can catch some very large moves; however, it has many of the same limitations that are inherent in the use of traditional moving averages.

Directional Movement Indicator (DMI) and Average Directional Movement Indicator (ADX)

These are unique indicators based on reasonable solid theories about market movement. They are calculated with relative ease and may be used either objectively as part of a trading system, or as trend and market strength indicators. ADX is a derivative of the directional movement indicator. It measures the *strength* of a market trend, not its direction. The higher the ADX, the more "directional" the market. The lower the ADX, the less "directional" the market. ADX does not measure whether a stock is rising or falling. The Overbought/Oversold (OB/OS) parameter sets boundaries on the strength or weakness of the *trend*, rather than on the strength or weakness of the *stock itself.*

Strengths

These methods are not based on effete concepts or market myths. They are well worth investigating for development into trading systems. The ADX and DMI are not used by many traders. Their main focus is on the strength of a trend and, as a result, they are somewhat different in their approach. Both timing methods can be very helpful when used in conjunction with other timing indicators.

Weaknesses

ADX and DMI tend to lag somewhat behind market tops and bottoms. As a result, they can give signals that may be somewhat late.

Momentum and/or Rate of Change (ROC)

These indicators are actually one and the same in the final analysis. Although they are derived from using different mathematical operations, their output is the same in terms of highs, lows, and trends. I believe that both momentum and ROC have been ignored and underrated as trading indicators and as valid inputs for trading systems. When momentum crosses above its zero line from a negative reading, a stock is considered to be in a bull trend. When momentum crosses below zero from a positive reading, the stock is considered to be in a bear trend. Momentum can be used in any time frame (that is, daily, intraday, weekly, and so forth).

STRENGTHS

- These indicators are very adaptable. They can be used not only as indicators but also can be developed into specific trading systems with risk management.
- They can be used with other indicators, such as moving average of the momentum.

WEAKNESSES

- Both indicators lag behind market turns to a given extent. As a result, they tend to be a little late at tops and bottoms.

For examples see Figures 5.5 and 5.6.

FIGURE 5.5 28-Day Momentum versus Price

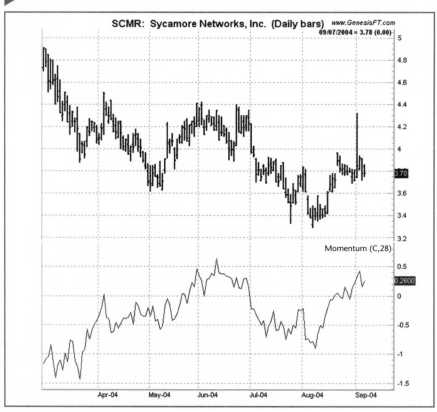

FIGURE 5.6 — Momentum/Moving Average Indicator Buy and Sell Signals

Accumulation Distribution and Its Derivative

This indicator is one of the more important ones for the stock trader. All market movements are a function of the ongoing struggle between those who are bullish and those who are bearish. While the bulls have buying power behind them, the bears have the power of selling pressure.

As long as buyers and sellers remain in balance with no group having clear control, prices remain in limbo, oscillating back and forth but not exhibiting any clear direction. At some point, however,

one group gains a clear upper hand, and the trend makes a con-
certed move in that direction.

For many years, traders have attempted to find a method that
would give insight into focus of control in a market. Clearly, if we
can know which group is in "control," we can buy or sell accordingly, with a relatively high degree of probability that we will be
right.

An example of the Williams Accumulation-Distribution
Indicator is shown in Figure 5.7.

FIGURE 5.7 Williams Accumulation-Distribution Indicator

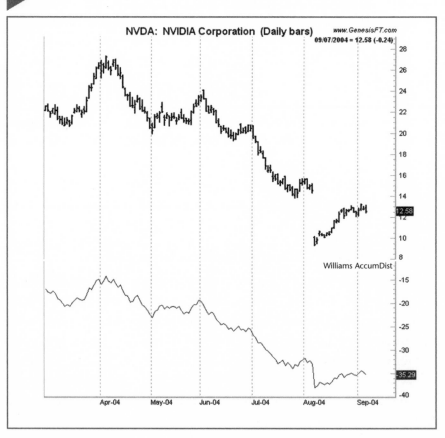

By "control" I mean the "balance of power." The question as to whether the bulls or the bears are "in control" of a market is an important one, particularly for the day trader. If we know that the bulls are in control of a market, then we will do well to buy on declines, knowing that the market is likely to recover from its drop. Buying on declines is not a simple matter. There are specific points at which we will want to buy on declines in a market that is in the firm control of the bulls. These will be delineated in our discussion of support and resistance.

In a market that is controlled by the bears, rallies will be relatively short-lived as sellers overpower buyers and the market returns to its declining trend. By *control*, we do not mean to imply that there is an actual group of buyers or sellers who are conspiring to control the direction of a market. By control, we mean essentially "balance of power." In such a market we will want to be sellers at resistance.

In a perfect world we would like to see markets follow our model or theory as closely as possible. While this would simplify our task as traders, it would likely mean an end to free markets, since virtually every market trend and trend change would be predictable and there would, therefore, be no markets. Yet, we know that this is not the case.

Given the imperfect state of affairs in the stock and futures markets, it would be advantageous to have available to us any indicators or systems that reveal the balance of power in a given market. For the stock trader, such a method would likely prove very profitable if correctly employed.

How could such a method work, and what measure of buying or selling power can we use to assist in our task as day traders? Theoretically, as a stock that has been in a bull trend begins to move sideways or makes an abrupt top, a change of control is taking place as the bears gain the upper hand over the bulls. One interpretation is that selling pressures outweigh buying power. Prices begin to turn lower, yet there is likely advance indication that this is about to happen.

During and prior to a sideways phase, the bears are "distributing" contracts to the bulls. The bulls eventually reach a point where their cumulative buying can no longer sustain an uptrend, and the market drops as the bears continue their selling. Hence, we call this phase *distribution*.

At a market bottom the reverse holds true. Accumulation takes place as the bulls gain the upper hand, overpowering selling by the bears. In theory, buying power outweighs the selling pressure. There is cumulatively more buying than selling. Eventually the balance is

FIGURE 5.8 ▶ Williams Accumulation/Distribution Moving Average

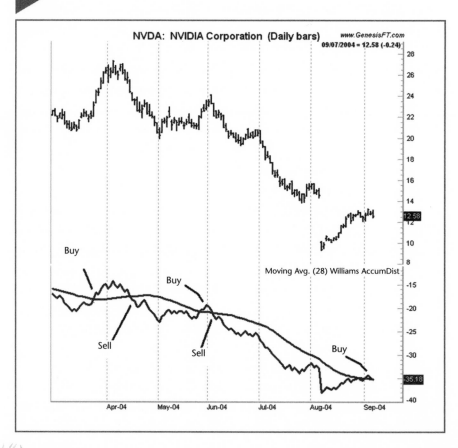

5 +1.3	BL		InTE	9.69	+.04 +2.1	IM		FF2010n	13.12	-.07 +1.4	BL		FndofAmY	25.20	-.14 +5.0	MC		MgSecs	1
3 +2.5	IL		MgdIn	9.35	+.02 +4.0	AB		FF2020n	13.07	-.11 +1.0	XC		GlobalA	35.41	+.07 +6.3	GL		SmlCapGro	1
9 +.9	BL		STGvSec	7.11	+1.1	SU		FF2030n	12.99	-.14 +.5	XC		OverseasA	19.59	+.04 +7.8	IL		SmallCo	1

overcome as buying demand outpaces the supply of selling, and the market surges higher. The bulls gain firm control, and prices move higher.

Theoretically, the bulls are slowly but surely gaining control of the market during the bottoming or "accumulation" phase. In spite of our wonderful theories and their face validity, stocks do not always conform to their ideal situations. At times, a stock will change trend almost immediately and seemingly without notice. Purists will argue that in such cases markets do give advance warnings but that the signs are subtle. We agree. But note that if the signs cannot be found, then the theory, no matter how seemingly valid, will not help us.

Figure 5.8 shows how the AD indicator is used with its moving average for timing.

Other Technical Indicators

Perhaps you did not find your favorite indicators included in the section above. Know that what you just read is intended to serve as a general introduction. There is much more technical information to follow. If we consider all of the timing indicators that have been developed over the years, as well as the many variations on the theme of these signals, there are literally thousands of possibilities that confront the short-term trader.

While it's true that the majority of these indicators are either useless or specious, there are some that can prove very valuable to the stock day trader. Our goal is to alert you to those that we believe to be effective, to show how they can be used. In the chapters that follow, we will employ some of the indicators discussed above as the core of specific trading systems and methods. We hope these will assist you in your goal of day trading for profits.

▶ Elements of an Effective Stock-Trading System

An effective trading system contains all the necessary elements in my STF trading model. This is the highest and most specific level of trading approaches. As noted in the previous discussion on trading systems, a trading system provides features that make it preferable to all other methods of trading. An effective system will tell you which stock to trade, when to buy, when to sell, how much to risk, and much more. While some traders prefer to use indicators and methods as opposed to systems, we believe that using a system will give you the greatest odds of success.

Here are the essential elements that an effective stock day-trading system must contain (factors also apply to trading systems that seek to capture longer-term moves as well):

- It contains purely objective rules for market entry and exit.
- It contains risk management rules, such as stop-loss and trailing stop-loss.
- It tells you which stocks to trade, and when to trade them.
- In can be back-tested to test its validity using the indicated rules.
- Its signals are not subject to interpretations—they are operational, totally objective, specific, and repeatable.
- Historical back-test performance provides key statistics and hypothetical results.
- Different traders should be able to get exactly the same signals using similar inputs.

There are other fine details that characterize a trading system; however, those indicated above are the most important. Clearly, the good news about trading systems is that they can be implemented specifically and without interpretation. The bad news is that many stock day traders are unable to follow a trading system due to their lack of discipline. They would much rather wallow in subjective indicators than have the self-confidence and self-discipline to trade a mechanical system. This book will present several day-trading systems for stocks; yet no matter how good they may look on paper or in back-testing, they will prove totally useless or even unprofitable to the trader who lacks discipline and consistency.

5 +1.3	BL	IntTE	9.89	+.04	+2.1	IM	FF2010n	13.12	-.07	+1.4	BL	FndofAmY	25.20	-.14	+5.0	MC
3 +2.5	IL	Mgdln	9.35	+.02	+4.0	AB	FF2020n	13.07	-.11	+1.0	XC	GlobalA	35.41	+.07	+6.3	GL
9 +.9	BL	STGvSec	7.11		+1.1	SU	FF2030n	12.99	-.14	+.5	XC	OverseasA	19.59	+.04	+7.8	IL

▶ Support and Resistance

Perhaps the single most valuable tool that a day trader can possess is the ability to determine support and resistance. My working definition of *support* as it applies to trading is as follows: The price level at which a market is expected to halt its declining trend and from which prices are expected to move higher at best, or sideways at worst.

As you can see, this is a purely pragmatic definition. It is tailor-made to the task at hand. But we hasten to add that support, in and of itself, is not particularly useful unless it is combined with knowledge of the existing trend. In an uptrend, the support level of a stock is likely to halt a short-term decline. Market technicians have developed numerous ways in which to determine support. The most common of these is to draw support trend lines under the price of a stock. While this can be effective, it is too subjective and often fails to provide sufficient information.

Other methods for determining support are based on percentage retracements, moving averages, previous highs and lows, reversal levels, waves, angles, Fibonacci numbers, markets geometry, and a host of other methods, some seemingly logical and others that smack of superstition or magic.

We will avoid most of the common and popular methods in favor of several that I have developed over the past 30 years, which I believe are highly effective. However, we do not expect you to take my word as gospel. We suggest that you critically evaluate my methods by watching them and seeing for yourself whether they can be helpful to you in your trading.

Conversely, resistance is an important consideration in a down-trending market. For our purposes, *resistance* is defined as follows: The price level at which a market is expected to halt its upward trend and from which prices are expected to move lower at worst, or sideways at best.

As in the case of support, there are literally hundreds of ways for determining resistance that traders have developed. Most of them are ineffective. Yet we must remember that the use of resistance (and support) is typically part of a trading method and not always systematic. Hence, a profitable outcome using resistance and support is, to a great extent, a function of the trader's skill level and experience.

▶ The Value of Trading with Support and Resistance

Support and resistance are valuable tools for the day trader. Knowing support and resistance levels, as well as the existing trend, can allow the day trader to accomplish the following goals:

- To buy, at or near support, in an uptrending market and to take profit either at a predetermined objective or at resistance
- To sell short, at or near resistance, in a downtrending market and to take profit either at a predetermined objective or at support
- To avoid markets that are trendless, or whose trading range is insufficient to allow reasonable intraday price movement
- To buy a market when it overcomes resistance and, therefore, go for a larger profit inasmuch as the uptrend is likely to remain strong because resistance has been overcome
- To sell a market when it falls below support and, therefore, to go for a larger profit because the downtrend is likely to remain strong now that support has been penetrated

To achieve these goals, the trader will need to know as precisely as possible, and with as much accuracy as possible, the current trend, the current support level, the current resistance level, and when a change in trend has taken place.

While these seem simple enough, they are lofty goals and not easily attained unless one uses the right methods. A good portion of what follows in this book will address the essential issues I have cited.

CHAPTER 6

Gap Your Way
to Profits

Now that you have been introduced to the TA method, let's forge ahead with the first of five methods I will teach you in this book. In every case I will tell you how the method works, why it works, how to implement it, when to implement it, its good points and its bad points. I hope that once you have completed your reading and studying, you will determine which method or methods are best for you. There is no single system,

05 +1.3	BL	IntTE	9.69	+.04 +2.1	IM	FF2010 n	13.12	−.07 +1.4	BL	FndofAmY	25.20	−.14 +5.0	MC	MydSets
03 +2.5	IL	Mgdln	9.35	+.02 +4.0	AB	FF2020 n	13.07	−.11 +1.0	XC	GlobalA	35.41	+.07 +6.3	GL	SmlCapGr
09 +.9	BL	STGvSec	7.11	+1.1	SU	FF2030 n	12.99	−.14 +.5	XC	OverseasA	19.59	+.04 +7.8	IL	SmallCo
10 +.3	XC									SoGenGold n15.85	+.55 −9.0	ALL	USGovSec

method, or approach to investing that will be right for all investors. There is no system method or indicator that will appeal to everyone. You'll need to "try things on for size." Some methods are more risky than others, but they are also more potentially profitable. Some methods are conservative but they also tend to yield smaller profits. Discover what fits you best and use it!

▶ Trading the Gap

One of the most basic and wonderful methods I know is the gap trade(GT). I cannot claim credit for developing this method, but I have made some important changes to it. The gap method (GM) was originally taught to me by Larry Williams, the well-known stock and commodity trader. Larry has written a number of excellent books about the markets that you may want to read if you're a serious investor or trader. If you are a short-term investor (otherwise known as a trader), this is a method that will have great appeal to you. I say this because typically this method will get you into and out of a trade in a matter of one to five days. This short-term approach, by its very nature, tends to yield smaller profits; however, always remember that the shorter the amount of time you are in a stock, the less money you can make—unless you trade a larger number of shares. It's only logical.

Trading gap appeals to me because it is quick and totally objective. But it has even deeper appeal to me because it is based on the psychological principles of fear and greed. These are the two most enduring causes of price movement in the stock market. Here is how they work.

Emotions and Prices

Investors and traders are fickle. This is no surprise inasmuch as most individuals are emotional when it comes to money. The more money involved, the more emotional the individual will be.

Investors who have their life savings at stake in the stock market can be highly emotional, often making the WRONG decisions. They tend to buy stocks when prices are high and to sell stocks when prices are low. Professional investors thrive on the emotional reactions of the public. When the public panics, professionals are there to take advantage of the profits that are the result of their having made the right moves at the right times. Although most investors are well aware that emotional decisions can be costly, many can't seem to change their behaviors. They consistently sell

 FIGURE 6.1 Example of Panic at the Bottom

Panic-selling engulfs this stock as it opens on a substantial gap BELOW its previous day's low. Note that not all gap lower openings signal bottoms.

FIGURE 6.2 ▶ Example of Panic at the Top

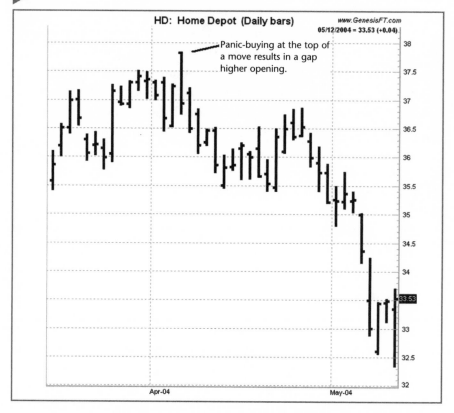

stocks at lows and buy stocks at highs. The gap trade is designed to take advantage of emotional selling and emotional buying.

Panic-buying at the top of a market trend tends to be characterized by a gap higher opening. The failed gap results in a sell signal per the gap method. Figures 6.1 and 6.2, respectively, illustrate these two conditions.

Common Features

The preceding examples have a common feature. They both developed after opening price gaps. In other words, it was the opening of the given stocks that alerted us to potentially profitable opportunities. Once the opening price was known, it was easy to determine our strategy.

▶ What Is the Opening Price?

Every stock has four important prices every day. These are the opening price, the closing price, the high price, and the low price. Indeed, there may be many prices in between, but these are the only four prices we are concerned about when using the GM. Here are some important definitions:

- *Opening price*. The very first price of the trading day. This is the price at which the first transaction of the day occurs. Note that many stocks can be traded 24 hours a day. The 24-hour trading does NOT interest us. We are only interested in the day-session trading which begins at 9 A.M. Central Time and ends at 3 P.M. Central Time. The opening price (also called the "open") is known almost immediately when the stock market begins trading. The open can be obtained from your broker, from any of the quotation services, or from your trading software that features live quotes. By "live quotes" I mean price quotations that are known as they develop in actual trading. Many quotations systems offer delayed quotes. Some of the delays can be as much as 30 minutes. DO NOT USE delayed quotes for this method. You must use live quotes only.

- *Close price*. This is also known as the "close," "closing price," "last price," "last," "settlement price," "settle," or the "ending price." This is the very last price that a stock has traded at when the day session is over. This price is important in helping us determine our profit or loss for the day.

- *High price*. Also know as the "high," "high of day," or the "day's high." This is the highest price at which a stock has traded during the day session.

.05 +1.3	BL	IntTE	9.69	+.04 +2.1	IM	FF2010n	13.12	-.07 +1.4	BL	FndofAmY	25.20	-.14 +5.0	MC	MyoeUS	
.03 +2.5	IL	Mgdin	8.35	+.02 +4.0	AB	FF2020n	13.07	-.11 +1.0	XC	GlobalA	35.41	+.07 +6.3	GL	SmlCapGr
.09 +.9	BL	STGvSec	7.11	+.1	SU	FF2030n	12.99	-.14 +.5	XC	OverseasA	19.59	+.04 +7.8	IL	SmlCo
.10 +.3	XC									SoGenGold n15.85	+.55 -9.0	ALL	USGovSec

- *Low price.* Also know as the "low," "low of day," or the "day's low." This is the lowest price at which a stock has traded during the day session.

All the above prices are available to you. In order to use the GM, you will need to know these prices. Rest assured that obtaining them is simple. If you have an online trading account, you can get these prices by logging in to your account. Alternatively, you can get these prices from your broker. There are many web sites where these prices can be obtained free of charge, but they may be delayed. Some prices are also available on business television, but these may also be delayed and will not be useful in implementing this method.

▶ How Gaps Look

A price gap occurs when the opening price of a stock is either BELOW the LOW of the previous day or ABOVE the HIGH of the previous day. Figure 6.3 shows gaps up and gaps down.

Now that you can identify gaps on a chart, let's look at what causes them to occur.

▶ What Causes Gaps?

Price gaps occur as a function of news. Bad news (i.e., bearish news) after the day session close of the stock market often causes a gap lower opening. Good news (i.e., bullish news) after the close of the day session in stocks often causes a gap higher opening. Gaps are indicators of emotional reactions by investors. These reactions are important because investors tend to panic at market extremes. As traders, we want to take advantage of the panic because emotional decisions are often (but not always) wrong decisions in the markets.

The above statements are somewhat general. Consider the following actual causes of price gaps in stocks or in the stock market in general:

FIGURE 6.3 ▶ Gap Up (U) and Gap Down (D) Days in GE Stock

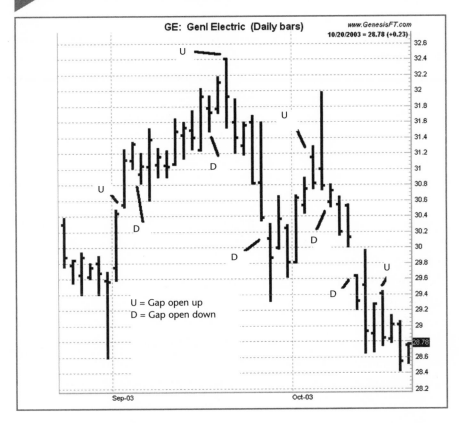

Event	Market Reaction
Federal Reserve raises interest rates unexpectedly.	Gap lower open
Three banks declare insolvency.	Gap lower open
IBM announces much better earnings than expected.	Gap higher open
OPEC raises crude oil production more than expected.	Gap lower open
Terrorists attack major financial institution.	Gap lower open
Leading economic indicators are very positive.	Gap higher open
Peace treaty is reached in the Middle East.	Gap higher open
Major world leader is assassinated.	Gap lower open
Company announces lower earnings than expected.	Gap lower open
CEO of a company is indicted for fraud.	Gap lower open
Weather causes severe damage in some areas.	Gap lower open

05 +1.3	BL	IntlTE	9.69	+.04 +2.1	IM	FF2010n	13.12	−.07 +1.4	BL	FndofAmY	25.20	−.14 +5.0	MC	MyoOus
03 +2.5	IL	Mgdln	9.35	+.02 +4.0	AB	FF2020n	13.07	−.11 +1.0	XC	GlobalA	35.41	+.07 +6.3	GL	SmtCapGr
09 +.9	BL	STGvSec	7.11	+.1.1	SU	FF2030n	12.99	−.14 +.5	XC	OverseasA	19.59	+.04 +7.8	IL	SmallCo
10 +.3	XC									SoGenGold n15.85		+.55 −9.0	ALI	USGovSec

These are just a few of the actual causes of gap openings. Remember that when the investing public responds to such news events, their reactions are a matter of interpretation. What appears to be negative news at first might actually be positive news in the long run. When selling or buying panic is pervasive, stocks move sharply up or down, respectively. When this happens, many professional traders try to take advantage of the panic by moving into the markets to either buy stocks that are selling at too low a price, or to sell short stocks that are trading at too high a price.

A Short-Term Game

As you can imagine, the effect of emotional responses in the marketplace is not long-lived. Typically, emotional reactions that cause opening gaps last through the end of the trading day. This is why the gap method is a useful tool for day trading. Before you rush to judgment, however, note that I am NOT suggesting that you become a day trader. There was a time when day trading was a viable venture (and adventure) for many individuals; however, that day is no longer. Even though I wrote one of the bestselling books on day trading in stocks (*The Compleat Guide to Day Trading Stocks*), I do not advocate such trading unless markets are moving in large daily ranges. The gap method is not the typical day trading method since it only makes one trade per day. Typically, day traders make many trades a day, seeking to make small profits on a large number of shares. The gap method seeks to make a larger amount of money on only one transaction.

▶ A Close Look at the Gap Trade Rules

I indicated above that the gap trade is a short-term game. As a result, gap trades are exited at the end of each day. There are some conditions under which you may want to keep a gap trade beyond the end of the trading day. These will be discussed later in this chapter. First, however, let's look at the GT rules of implementation.

Within the structure of my Setup, Trigger, and Follow-Through method, here are the rules of the gap trade.

Gap Trade Buy Setup

If a stock OPENS below the low of the previous day, then a gap-buy situation has developed. On a price chart the GT buy set-up looks like Figure 6.4

FIGURE 6.4 GT Buy Setup

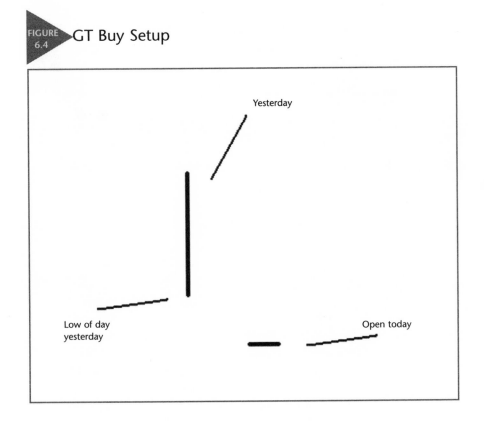

Trigger for Gap Buy Trade

Once the stock has opened below the low of the previous day and sets up a possible buy trigger, the stock must go back up and penetrate the low of the previous day in order to trigger a buy signal. The amount by which a stock penetrates the low of the previous

FIGURE 6.5 Gap Buy Trades in Sina

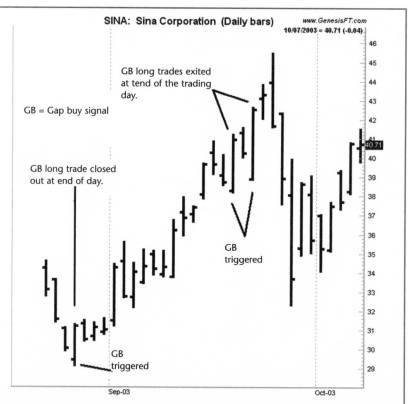

This chart shows three GB signals that were closed out at the end of the day at a profit. There were several other gaps, but the size of the opening gap was not large enough to trigger a buy signal. Note that I have NOT marked the sell gaps on this chart in order to keep from complicating matters. The sell gap signals will be discussed and illustrated later in this chapter.

day is important and CAN make a difference in bottom-line performance. Figure 6.5 shows examples of gap-trade buy signals that have triggered. See my notes on the chart.

Now let's take a close look at exactly how a GB is triggered. Figure 6.6 shows a typical GB signal from start to finish

A gap sell signal occurs when a stock opens above the previous day's high and drops below it. Figure 6.7 shows this pattern.

Now take a look at Figure 6.8, which shows GB signals in MSFT. I marked each of the gap buy signals. As you can see, there

FIGURE 6.6 ▶ Gap Lower Opening and by Trigger

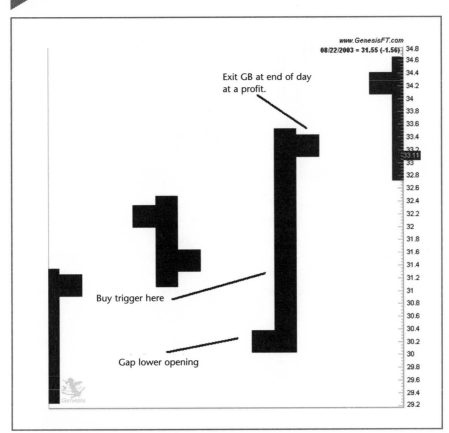

Gap Sell Trades

FIGURE 6.7

YHOO: Yahoo! Inc. (Daily bars)

www.GenesisFT.com
08/31/2004 = 28.51 (+0.05)

Three gap sell signals in YHOO, each of which triggered. Gaps A and B both closed out at the end of the day at a relatively large profit. Gap C closed out at the end of the day at a small profit. Close each day was at or near the low of the day.

This chart shows a GS (gap sell) signal from start to finish. A gap higher opening was the setup for a sell trade that triggered a short position by coming back into the range of the previous day. The trade then followed through to the downside and was closed out at the end of the day at a profit. This is the typical gap sell trade. Not all GB trades will have the same profitable result; however, the GB is a very reliable signal that is ideal for day traders. Note gap sell signals at points A, B, and C.

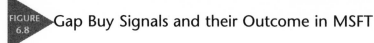

Gap Buy Signals and their Outcome in MSFT

FIGURE 6.8

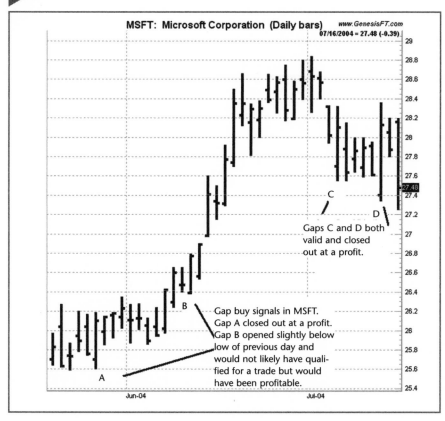

are not too many GB signals, but those that do occur tend to be profitable. Note also that there are several GS signals that I have not marked to keep from complicating matters, and because I would like you to focus on the GS signals and their outcomes.

Figures 6.9 and 6.10 illustrate several signals in different stocks.

FIGURE 6.9 Gap Sell Trades in SMTC

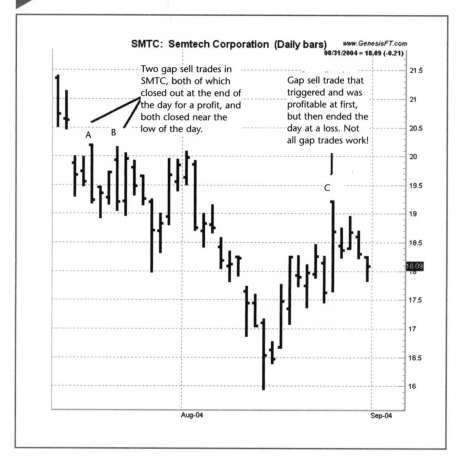

SMTC: Semtech Corporation (Daily bars)   www.GenesisFT.com
08/31/2004 = 18.09 (-0.21)

Two gap sell trades in SMTC, both of which closed out at the end of the day for a profit, and both closed near the low of the day.

Gap sell trade that triggered and was profitable at first, but then ended the day at a loss. Not all gap trades work!

FIGURE
6.10

Gap Buy Trades in Newmont Mining

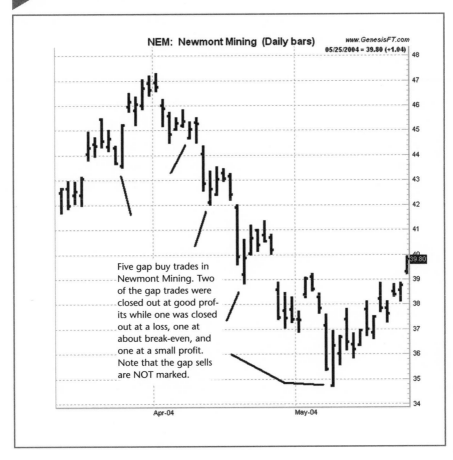

Five gap buy trades in Newmont Mining. Two of the gap trades were closed out at good profits while one was closed out at a loss, one at about break-even, and one at a small profit. Note that the gap sells are NOT marked.

05	+1.3	BL		IntTE	9.69	+.04	+2.1	IM	FF2010n	13.12	-.07	+1.4	BL	FndofAmY	25.20	-.14	+5.0	MC	MySec
03	+2.5	IL		Mgdln	9.35	+.02	+4.0	AB	FF2020n	13.07	-.11	+1.0	XC	GlobalA	35.41	+.07	+6.3	GL	SmlCapGr
09	+.9	BL		STGvSec	7.11		+1.1	SU	FF2030n	12.99	-.14	+.5	XC	OverseasA	19.59	+.04	+7.8	IL	SmallCo
10	+.3	XC												SoGenGold n15.85	+.55	-9.0	AU	USGovSec

Gap Trade Sell Setup

If a stock OPENS above the high of the previous day, then a sell setup has happened. Example, on a price chart, the GT sell setup looks like Figure 6.11.

Trigger for Gap Sell Trade

Once the stock has opened above the high of the previous day and sets up a possible sell trigger, the stock must go back down and penetrate the high of the previous day in order to trigger a sell signal (see Figure 6.11). The amount by which a stock penetrates the high of the previous day is important and CAN make a difference

FIGURE 6.11 GT Higher Opening

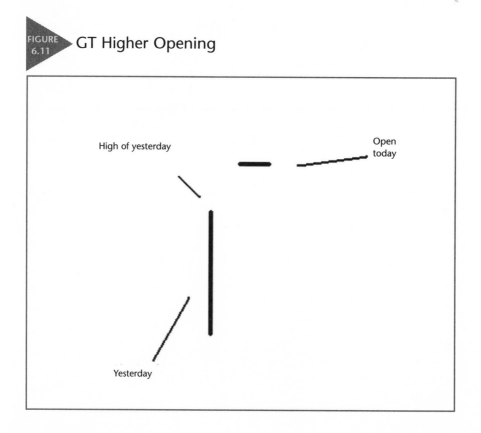

in bottom-line performance. Figure 6.12 shows examples of gap-trade sell signals that have triggered. See my notes on the chart.

Now take a close look at exactly how a GS is triggered. Figure 6.13 shows a typical GS signal from start to finish.

◤FIGURE 6.12 ▶ Examples of Three Gap Sell Signals

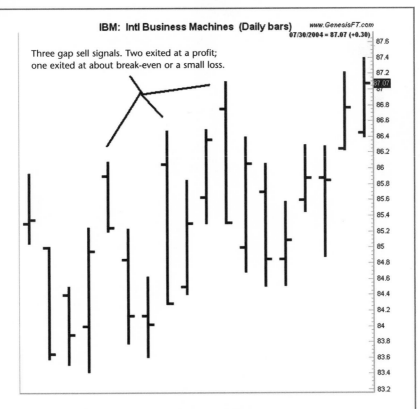

This chart shows three GS signals that were closed out at the end of the day at a profit. There were several other gaps but the size of the opening gap was not large enough to trigger a buy signal. Note that to keep from complicating matters, I have NOT marked the sell gaps on this chart.

FIGURE 6.13 ▸ Gap Sell Signal from Start to Finish

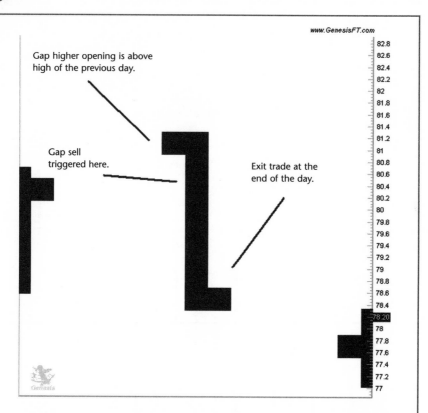

This chart shows a GS signal from start to finish. A gap higher opening was the setup for a sell trade that triggered a short position by falling back into the range of the previous day. The trade then followed through to the downside and was closed out at the end of the day at a profit. This is the typical gap sell trade. Not all GS trades will have the same profitable result; however, the GS is a very reliable signal that is ideal for day traders.

Now take a look at Figures 6.14 and 6.15, which show GS signals in several stocks. I have marked each of the gap sell signals with a GS. As you can see, there are not too many GS signals, but those that do occur tend to be profitable.

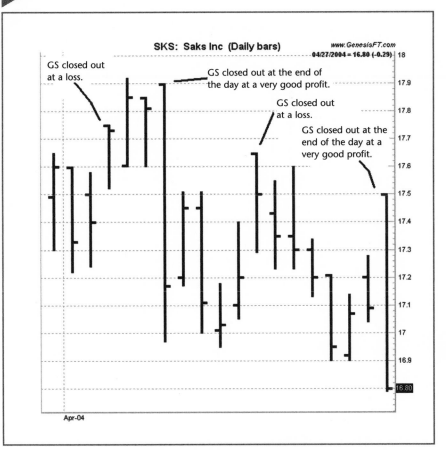

FIGURE 6.14 ▶ Gap Sell Signals in SKS

FIGURE 6.15 Gap Sell Signals in OI

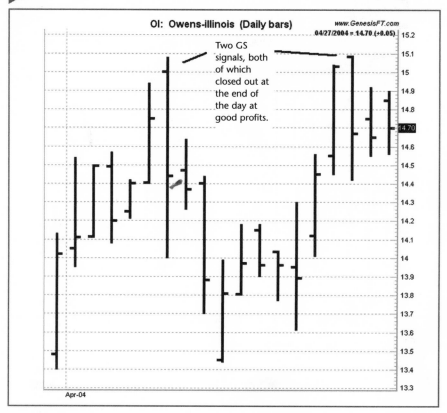

OI: Owens-illinois (Daily bars)

Two GS signals, both of which closed out at the end of the day at good profits.

▶ Gap Size and Penetration Amount

There are two important variables that must be considered when trading the gap buy and sell signals. They are

1. Size of the opening gap, and
2. Penetration amount for long and short entries.

Size of the Opening Gap

This variable is the amount that the stock opens ABOVE the highs of the previous day or BELOW the low of the previous day. The bigger the opening gap, the less likelihood there is that the gap trade will actually trigger. If, however, a gap trade DOES trigger on a large opening gap, then the odds of a profitable trade are good. Stated simply, "the bigger the gap, the better the trade." Different gap opening sizes yield different results. To find the best size of a gap in a given stock, you will need to do a little research. Generally, a gap of about one-fourth of 1 percent of the price of the stock is a good rule of thumb to use for gap size.

As an example, see Table 6.1, which gives the results of a gap trade in the stock of IBM using several different opening gap sizes.

TABLE 6.1

IBM 1998–2004. Gap open 20 cents above previous daily high or gap open 10 cents below previous daily low; penetration of 35 cents back into high of previous day and penetration of 50 cents into previous daily low. Exit on first profitable opening with 3.9 percent stop loss below entry price.

Summary—All Trades Report

Aug 14, 2004 16:15:51

Name: Gap Trade
Symbol: IBM 2000-2004
Position selection: All trades, From date 01/20/2000, To date 07/23/2004, Chart By Date, Ignore trades <= -999,999, Ignore trades >= 999,999, Ignore big wins 0, Ignore big losses 0, Profit is >= 0.00, Show cents No, Show Max Intra No, MA Type Simple, MA Periods 1

Overall

Total Net Profit:	$52,650	Profit Factor ($Wins/$Losses):	2.50
Total Trades:	119	Winning Percentage:	84.0%
Average Trade:	$442	Payout Ratio (Avg Win/Loss):	0.47
Avg # of Bars in Trade:	1.55	Z-Score (W/L Predictability):	8.8
Avg # of Trades per Year:	26.4	Percent in the Market:	13.1%
Max Closed-out Drawdown:	-$6,605	Max Intraday Drawdown:	-$6,605
Account Size Required:	$6,605	Return Pct:	797.1%
Open Equity:	$0	Kelly Ratio:	0.5037
Current Streak:	2 Wins	Optimal f:	0.52

TABLE 6.1,cont				
Winning Trades		**Losing Trades**		
Total Winners:	100	Total Losers:		19
Gross Profit:	$87,845	Gross Loss:		-$35,195
Average Win:	$878	Average Loss:		-$1,852
Largest Win:	$6,595	Largest Loss:		-$2,375
Largest Drawdown in Win:	-$2,025	Largest Peak in Loss:		$1,625
Avg Drawdown in Win:	-$231	Avg Peak in Loss:		$308
Avg Run Up in Win:	$1,064	Avg Run Up in Loss:		$308
Avg Run Down in Win:	-$231	Avg Run Down in Loss:		-$1,884
Most Consec Wins:	18	Most Consec Losses:		3
Avg # of Consec Wins:	3.33	Avg # of Consec Losses:		0.68
Avg # of Bars in Wins:	1.47	Avg # of Bars in Losses:		1.95

As you can see, the test results are impressive, with 84 percent of the trades being profitable. I have deducted $25 per round turn commission. These results assume a 500 share position.

Penetration Amount

Now take a look at the same stock with the same rules except for a change in the variables noted in Table 6.2. In other words, let's look at the same method but let's vary the size of the opening gap as well as the size of the penetration amount for long and short entries.

As you can see from the historical test results shown in Table 6.2, these are critically important variables. Different values can produce markedly different results. To determine which results are best, you can test different amounts using a computer program that is designed to test out the different values, giving you the best historical results. This process, known as optimization, is an excellent tool as long as it is used wisely. By optimizing the possible inputs in increments that are too small, you can create a wonderful system that would have worked with stellar results in the past but which will not go forward in real time with similar results.

TABLE 6.2

Summary—All Trades Report

Aug 14, 2004 16:39:13

Name: Gap trade IBM 2

Symbol: IBM 2000-2004

Position selection: All trades, From date 01/20/2000, To date 06/09/2004, Chart By Date, Ignore trades <= -999,999, Ignore trades >= 999,999, Ignore big wins 0, Ignore big losses 0, Profit is >= 0.00, Show cents No, Show Max Intra No, MA Type Simple, MA Periods 1

Overall

Total Net Profit:	$41,510	Profit Factor ($Wins/$Losses):	5.25
Total Trades:	56	Winning Percentage:	92.9%
Average Trade:	$741	Payout Ratio (Avg Win/Loss):	0.40
Avg # of Bars in Trade:	2.16	Z-Score (W/L Predictability):	1.1
Avg # of Trades per Year:	12.8	Percent in the Market:	8.6%
Max Closed-out Drawdown:	-$2,885	Max Intraday Drawdown:	-$5,090
Account Size Required:	$5,090	Return Pct:	815.5%
Open Equity:	$0	Kelly Ratio:	0.7517
Current Streak:	10 Wins	Optimal f:	0.79

Winning Trades		Losing Trades	
Total Winners:	52	Total Losers:	4
Gross Profit:	$51,280	Gross Loss:	-$9,770
Average Win:	$986	Average Loss:	-$2,443
Largest Win:	$6,445	Largest Loss:	-$2,885
Largest Drawdown in Win:	-$2,450	Largest Peak in Loss:	$265
Avg Drawdown in Win:	-$382	Avg Peak in Loss:	$220
Avg Run Up in Win:	$1,221	Avg Run Up in Loss:	$220
Avg Run Down in Win:	-$382	Avg Run Down in Loss:	-$2,443
Most Consec Wins:	27	Most Consec Losses:	1
Avg # of Consec Wins:	10.40	Avg # of Consec Losses:	1.00
Avg # of Bars in Wins:	2.06	Avg # of Bars in Losses:	3.50

As you can see, the parameters used in this report have increased accuracy to over 90 percent while also increasing the average profit per trade and reducing the total number of trades.

05	+1.3	BL		IntTE	9.69	+.04	+2.1	IM		FF2010n	13.12	-.07	+1.4	BL		FndofAmY	25.20	-.14	+5.0	MC		MgSec
03	+2.5	IL		Mgdln	9.35	+.02	+4.0	AB		FF2020n	13.07	-.11	+1.0	XC		GlobalA	35.41	+.07	+6.3	GL		SmlCapGr
09	+.9	BL		STGvSec	7.11		+1.1	SU		FF2030n	12.99	-.14	+.5	XC		OverseasA	19.59	+.04	+7.8	IL		SmallCo
10	+.3	XC														SoGenGold n	15.85	+.55	-9.0	ALL		USGovSec

The values used are as follows:

Size of opening gap up: 30 cents
Size of opening gap down: 90 cents
Penetration down into previous daily high: 35 cents
Penetration up into previous daily low: 80 cents
Stop loss: 4.75 percent

As you can see, these variables produce different results. The key to trading gaps profitably is to find variables that are consistent with your finances, your temperament, and your investment or trading goals.

Table 6.3 looks at a few more historical records in another well-known stock to see how the GT method fared historically. As you can see from the following performance history, the gap method has performed well in e-Bay with over 87 percent accuracy.

Table 6.3 also shows gap trades in EBAY from 1990–2004. As you can see, the performance record has been impressive with respect to accuracy and the average profit per trade. The values used are as follows:

Size of opening gap up: 48 cents
Size of opening gap down: 48 cents
Penetration down into previous daily high: 4 cents
Penetration up into previous daily low: 98 cents
Stop loss: 3.55 percent

▶ Reviewing the Gap Method

Let's review the gap method trading rules as well as some important points about its implementation.

The gap method enters a LONG position if a stock has opened below the low of the previous day by more than a given amount and then enters back into the range of the previous day by penetrating back up through the low of the previous day by a given amount. The trade exists using a stop loss that is a percentage of the entry price or it takes profit on the first profitable opening.

TABLE 6.3

Summary—All Trades Report

Aug 16, 2004 07:00:32

Name: Gap Trade

Symbol: EBAY 1990-2004

Position selection: All trades, From date 11/30/1998, To date 07/23/2004, Chart By Date, Ignore trades <= -999,999, Ignore trades >= 999,999, Ignore big wins 0, Ignore big losses 0, Profit is >= 0.00, Show cents No, Show Max Intra No, MA Type Simple, MA Periods 1

Overall

Total Net Profit:	$27,145	Profit Factor ($Wins/$Losses):	8.19
Total Trades:	57	Winning Percentage:	87.7%
Average Trade:	$476	Payout Ratio (Avg Win/Loss):	1.15
Avg # of Bars in Trade:	1.30	Z-Score (W/L Predictability):	0.1
Avg # of Trades per Year:	10.1	Percent in the Market:	5.1%
Max Closed-out Drawdown:	-$1,025	Max Intraday Drawdown:	-$1,370
Account Size Required:	$1,370	Return Pct:	1,981.4%
Open Equity:	$0	Kelly Ratio:	0.7701
Current Streak:	18 Wins	Optimal f:	0.85

Winning Trades		**Losing Trades**	
Total Winners:	50	Total Losers:	7
Gross Profit:	$30,920	Gross Loss:	-$3,775
Average Win:	$618	Average Loss:	-$539
Largest Win:	$2,915	Largest Loss:	-$730
Largest Drawdown in Win:	-$445	Largest Peak in Loss:	$585
Avg Drawdown in Win:	-$88	Avg Peak in Loss:	$178
Avg Run Up in Win:	$823	Avg Run Up in Loss:	$178
Avg Run Down in Win:	-$88	Avg Run Down in Loss:	-$539
Most Consec Wins:	18	Most Consec Losses:	2
Avg # of Consec Wins:	7.14	Avg # of Consec Losses:	1.17
Avg # of Bars in Wins:	1.38	Avg # of Bars in Losses:	.71

The gap method enters a SHORT position if a stock has opened above the high of the previous day by more than a given amount and then enters back into the range of the previous day by penetrating back down through the high of the previous day by a given amount. The trade exists using a stop loss that is a percentage of the entry price or it takes profit on the first profitable opening.

The amount of the openong gap, the amount of the penetration, and the size of the stop loss are critical variables that must be determined for each stock you want to trade. You can accomplish this by using one of the various trading software programs that allow for such testing (i.e., Genesis Navigator Platinum) or by manually determining these levels (although this can be a formidable task).

The gap method is strictly a short-term method with trades usually lasting only one day. There are ways by which the holding period of the gap trade can be increased. Readers who are inclined to do market research on their trading strategies are urged to determine the ideal values for the stocks they are interested in trading.

Best performance is achieved by trading larger blocks of shares (i.e., 500 shares), because commission costs will constitute a smaller percentage of overall costs than if you trade a smaller number of shares.

The gap method is totally mechanical. By this I mean that signals for each trade are completely objective with regard to entry price, method of exit, stop loss, etc. No consideration whatsoever is given to the news, market fundamentals, market analyst opinions, or even your own opinions! If you intend to be successful with this method, or for that matter, any method discussed in this book, you will need to implement the trades mechanically, consistently, and with iron discipline.

▶ Multi-Gap Method

For those who are inclined to do more research, I offer a variation on the theme. I call it the multi-gap trade because rather than using a gap opening above or below the low or high of the previous day, it looks for opening gaps that are either above or below the high or low of a number of days. As an example, consider the following

FIGURE 6.16 ►Example of a Multi-Gap Up Opening

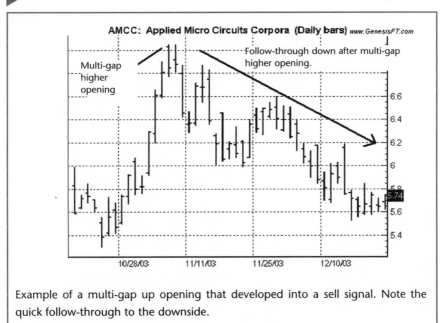

Example of a multi-gap up opening that developed into a sell signal. Note the quick follow-through to the downside.

(Figure 6.16). It shows a gap higher opening where the gap open is above the highest high of the last ten days (or more).

Such gaps tend to make for larger and more immediate moves than one-day gaps. The multi-gap sell trade looks for gap openings that are lower than the low of more than one day. Figure 6.17 shows such a gap. In addition to the multi-gap opening, this method can be adapted take profits on the "Nth profitable opening". By this I mean that profits can be increased by taking profit on multi-gap trade on a profitable opening that is longer than the first profitable opening exit used with one-day gap trades.

FIGURE 6.17

Example of a Multi-Gap Down Opening

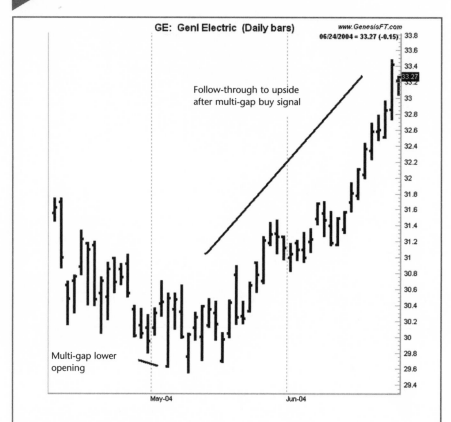

Example of a multi-gap down opening that developed into a buy signal. Note the lengthy follow-through to the upside.

Short-Term Key Date Seasonal Trades

 You are about to embark on a journey of seasonal discovery that may open your eyes to a whole new world of stock trading. In this chapter you will find a vast amount of information on seasonal trading in stocks. Seasonal trading in stocks is a very specific approach that can be used in a totally mechanical fashion. By "mechanical," I mean that the seasonal method I will teach you lends itself perfectly to the GIM and STF methods discussed earlier in this book.

Given my experience in the stock and commodity markets since 1968, I know what traders want, how traders trade, and how to provide you with trading methods that will help you profit, not only in the short run but in the long run as well. The seasonal approach is so thoroughly objective that it can be used by beginners as well as seasoned veterans. It answers virtually all the questions that can be asked about when to buy or sell, the odds of success, stop loss, profit objective, historical performance, and much more. Although it is by no means the only trading available, it is, in my view, one of the best because it lends itself readily to a fully objective, organized, and disciplined approach that fits well within the frameworks I have given you earlier.

Do Not Ignore the Risks

No matter how strongly I may sing the praises of seasonal trading, do not forget that profitable stock trading is as much a function of solid risk management and discipline as it is of good research and follow-through. No matter how good the seasonal patterns in this chapter may be, they will not bring profits unless they are implemented in a comprehensive program of risk management that limits its losses and maximizes profits. I hope you enjoy reading this chapter and using these seasonal methods, as much as I enjoyed writing it.

In closing, one caveat: **BEWARE OF MISLEADING SEASONAL RESEARCH.** There are various purveyors of seasonal research who offer for sale seasonal trades which appear to have an outstanding record of accuracy.

Some claim that many of their seasonal trades are 100 percent correct. And in this claim they are not misleading you. The other side of the coin, however, is that these "amazing" seasonals only contain from five to ten years of historical research. As you will see from what follows in this chapter, such a relatively short historical time frame cannot be relied upon to yield valid results.

Hence, seasonal trades based upon limited historical data are **NO BETTER THAN A TOSS OF THE COIN.**

Limited data history is one of the greatest drawbacks of seasonal trading. Even the seasonals I offer, which are based on years' worth of price history in some cases, are not as statistically valid as we would like them to be. Please do not fall victim to the outrageous claims of these operators! I assure you that following such "bogus" seasonals will cost you money, time and time again. As always, a word to the wise should be sufficient. Finally, remember that seasonal trades do not predict the future; they only tell us what has happened in the past. The more historical data we have in our sample, the more reliable will be our seasonal trades. Please remember this!

▶ What Is a Seasonal?

Most markets move in fairly regular price patterns. These patterns exist in the financial markets (i.e., stocks, commodities, and bonds) as well as economic data and many naturally occurring phenomena. To most traders these periodic movements are not meaningful, because they are usually not obvious. And this is truly unfortunate, because regularity and repetition are the cornerstones of profitable trading and investing. All trading systems, methods, and indicators seek to isolate signals or patterns which repeat themselves frequently enough and with sufficient reliability to permit profitable trading. Seasonals and cycles are the quintessential factors underlying market regularity. Those who have read my various books and articles on these topics should be familiar with the basic long-term cycles in each market.

Virtually all commodity and stock markets are affected by weather, season, and growing conditions. Supply and demand are a function of seasonal fluctuations. When crops are large following harvest, it would be natural to assume that prices may be low due to farmers' sales activity. When demand for grain is high, during winter months, we might expect prices to be high. But there are many other factors which affect prices. When consumers are influenced by weather to buy either more products or fewer products, the end result can have a marked effect on company profits which, in turn, affect earnings and therefore the selling price of their stocks. When the weather is hot and demand for electricity is high, fuel consumption to generate electricity increases, and with it the price of petroleum can rise. Rising petroleum prices can affect the earnings of petroleum producers and refiners, as well as petroleum equipment suppliers. This, in turn, affects the price of their shares. When a hurricane inflicts its devastating blow, destroying homes, buildings, and other property, demand for building supplies increases, thereby potentially boosting the earnings of companies that supply these goods. And the list of possibilities goes on.

Certainly all these factors, if known, would effect the errorless forecasting of prices. Our ability to recognize and utilize all the price variables is limited; hence, our forecasting ability is limited. Inasmuch as seasonal factors affect prices, it is possible, or should be, to determine if and when a given market will move up or down due to the season.

A seasonal pattern is, therefore, the tendency of a given market or stock to trend in a given direction at certain times of the year. We do not always know the reasons for seasonal price movements. Personally, I have no need to know why a market moves up or down at a given time of the year. Certainly, knowing 'why' makes some traders feel more secure. My concern is not with the **WHY** of things, but rather with the **THAT** of things.

Perhaps the earliest-known record of seasonals was presented by the sixth-century B.C. Greek philosopher Thales. Based on his understanding of astronomy, he was able to forecast a bumper crop of olives well in advance. Armed with this information, he acquired numerous olive presses in winter, when they were cheap. When the huge olive crop was harvested and demand for presses

5	+1.3	BL		IntTE	9.69	+.04	+2.1	IM		FF2010n	13.12	-.07	+1.4	BL		FndotAmY	25.20	-.14	+5.0	MC		MySecs
3	+2.5	IL		Mgdln	9.35	+.02	+4.0	AB		FF2020n	13.07	-.11	+1.0	XC		GlobalA	35.41	+.07	+6.3	GL		SmICapGro
9	+.9	BL		STGvSec	7.11		+1.1	SU		FF2030n	12.99	-.14	+.5	XC		OverseasA	19.59	+.04	+7.8	IL		SmallCo
	+3	XC														SoGenGold n15.85		+.55	-.9.0	ALL		USGovSecs

was high, he was able to command a high rental price and thus make a good profit. Traders have been using seasonality in its various forms for many years. Yet, there are some reasonable issues surrounding its use, as well as cogent challenges to the validity of seasonals.

W. D. Gann underscored the importance of seasonal price tendencies in commodity futures prices in his book, *How to Make Profits Trading in Commodities* (1942), where he devoted considerable attention to this concept. Today, with the assistance of computer technology, it is possible to determine accurately and with specificity most seasonal factors in the commodity futures markets as well as the stock market. Whereas Gann was primarily interested in using seasonal highs and lows in the commodity markets, the seasonal concept can be used to isolate patterns in individual stocks within specific calendar dates.

Do Stock and Commodity Prices Show Seasonal Price Variations?

I believe that the lengthy history of stock prices, cash commodity prices, and futures prices strongly supports the existence of seasonality. As an example, my intensive research on cash corn prices, where the database spans more than 276 years, fully supports the idea that prices show seasonal fluctuations. In addition, the highly valid statistical work of Arthur Merrill in his excellent book *The Behavior of Prices on Wall Street* (Analysis Press), presented hard statistical evidence that pre-holiday seasonal patterns exist in the stock market, and that they have shown a very high incidence of repetition.

Adding to the base of statistical validity in seasonals, extensive research by the Foundation for the Study of Cycles further validates the existence of seasonal price tendencies in the stock and commodity markets. Even the United States government, in calculating many of its economic indicators, factors in the effect of seasonality by using "seasonally adjusted" data. Hence, we know that the effects of seasonal behavior are clearly present and that they continue to exert an influence on prices as well as other economic variables.

As an example of seasonal price behavior in the stock market, consider the behavior of stock prices as measured by the Dow Jones Industrial Average between April 5 and April 25, 1970 to 2004 in Figure 7.1.

This pattern shows that the closing price of the Dow Jones Industrials has been higher on or about 4/22 than it was on or about 4/5 over 77 percent of the time since 1970. Although this pattern has not been perfect, it has been highly predictable. In addition to the high probability of occurrence, it has averaged a profit of over 3.1 percent when it was right as opposed to a loss of 2.01 percent when it was wrong. This is a clear-cut example of seasonality at its best. I call this pattern a "key date" seasonal.

▶ What Is Key-Date Seasonal Analysis?

Seasonal key-date analysis, a method I developed many years ago for the futures, has been extended to stocks. At a glance, key-date seasonal analysis of a stock will tell you virtually everything you need to know about a given trade or market. Key-date seasonals answer the following seven vital questions for the trader:

1. What stocks(s) to trade?
2. Whether to buy or sell?
3. The exact date to enter and exit?
4. The exact stop loss to use?
5. The complete performance history of the trade(s)?
6. The exact time of day to enter or exit?
7. The odds of success?

This important list can go a long way toward decreasing the number of losses and the dollar amount of each loss you take, by keeping you focused on a set of defined parameters, as provided

Seasonal Pattern in the Dow Jones Industrial Average from April 5 to April 25, 1970 to 2004

FIGURE 7.1

Entry Year	Date In	Price In	Date Out	Price Out	Profit/Loss	P/L Pct	Total P/L
1970	4/6	791.20	4/22	762.60	-28.60	-3.61	-28.60
1971	4/5	905.10	4/22	940.60	35.50	3.92	6.90
1972	4/5	954.60	4/24	957.50	2.90	0.30	9.80
1973	4/5	923.50	4/23	955.40	31.90	3.45	41.70
1974	4/5	847.50	4/22	858.60	11.10	1.30	52.80
1975	4/7	742.90	4/22	814.10	71.20	9.58	124.00
1976	4/5	1004.10	4/22	1007.70	3.60	0.35	127.60
1977	4/5	916.10	4/22	927.10	11.00	1.20	138.60
1978	4/5	763.10	4/24	826.10	63.00	8.25	201.60
1979	4/5	877.60	4/23	860.10	-17.50	-1.99	184.10
1980	4/7	768.30	4/22	789.80	21.50	2.79	205.60
1981	4/6	994.20	4/22	1007.00	12.80	1.28	218.40
1982	4/5	835.30	4/22	853.10	17.80	2.13	236.20
1983	4/5	1120.20	4/22	1196.30	76.10	6.79	312.30
1984	4/5	1130.50	4/23	1149.50	19.00	1.68	331.30
1985	4/8	1253.00	4/22	1266.60	13.60	1.08	344.90
1986	4/7	1735.50	4/22	1831.00	95.50	5.50	440.40
1987	4/6	2405.50	4/22	2285.90	-119.60	-4.97	320.80
1988	4/5	1997.50	4/22	2015.10	17.60	0.88	338.40
1989	4/5	2304.80	4/24	2402.70	97.90	4.24	436.30

FIGURE 7.1 Seasonal Pattern in the Dow Jones Industrial Average, continued

Entry Year	Date In	Price In	Date Out	Price Out	Profit/Loss	P/L Pct	Total P/L
1990	4/5	2721.20	4/23	2666.70	-54.50	-2.00	381.80
1991	4/5	2896.80	4/22	2927.70	30.90	1.06	412.70
1992	4/6	3275.50	4/22	3338.80	63.30	1.93	476.00
1993	4/5	3379.50	4/22	3429.20	49.70	1.47	525.70
1994	4/5	3675.40	4/22	3648.70	-26.70	-0.72	499.00
1995	4/5	4200.60	4/24	4304.00	103.40	2.46	602.40
1996	4/8	5594.40	4/22	5564.70	-29.70	-0.53	572.70
1997	4/7	6555.90	4/22	6833.60	277.70	4.23	850.40
1998	4/6	9033.20	4/22	9176.70	143.50	1.58	993.90
1999	4/5	10007.30	4/22	10721.80	714.50	7.13	1708.40
2000	4/5	11033.00	4/25	11124.80	91.80	0.83	1800.20
2001	4/5	9918.00	4/23	10532.20	614.20	6.19	2414.40
2002	4/5	10271.60	4/22	10136.40	-135.20	-1.31	2279.20
2003	4/7	8300.40	4/22	8485.00	184.60	2.22	2463.80
2004	4/5	10558.40	4/22	10461.20	-97.20	-0.92	2366.60

Trades: 35	Winners: 27	Losers: 8	% Winners: 77.14	Daily PF: 6.2649
Avg Prof: 106.5037	Avg Loss: -63.6250	% Avg Prof: 3.10	% Avg Loss: -2.01	

by the key-date rules. Key-date seasonal trading requires no judgment. It does not depend on ANY external sources of information, fundamental or technical. Key-date seasonal trades are very specific. According to my method, these trades are always entered on the close of trading and exited on the close of trading on the dates shown. The stop loss is a percentage of the price on day of entry.

If a stock is closed on the recommended entry or exit days, then you execute the seasonal trade on the close of trading, the next business day.

▶ Stop Losses

All stop losses for the seasonal stock trades are "close only." This means that if you are short, the market must close above the calculated stop loss. Obviously, you could, therefore, be stopped out at a loss that is greater than what you had intended. The same stop-loss rule applies for a long position. The close-only stop means that your position could be liquidated at a larger loss than what you had expected.

High-Accuracy, Short-Term, Key-Date Trades

The trades that follow are high-accuracy, key-date seasonals. They are among the most reliable of all seasonals I have ever found. Please note the following guide to reading the reports. *Note that trades that exited before the ideal exit date were stopped out at the indicated price.* Seasonals are not the Holy Grail of stock or futures trading. They are just as fallible as any other trading method.

Yet to me, seasonals represent a much more stable and sensible approach to trading because they are based on the well-established tendency for history to repeat. There is nothing as good as having the weight of history on your side. And that's what seasonals can do for you. But remember, no matter WHAT the seasonals say, you MUST exercise effective risk management if you want seasonals to work for you. ALWAYS limit losses. If you don't, you'll ride losses, which will eventually eat up all your profits and much, much more.

.05	+1.3	BL		IntTE	9.69	+.04	+2.1	IM		FF2010n	13.12	-.07	+1.4	BL		FndofAmY	25.20	-.14	+5.0	MC		MidSec5	
.03	+2.5	IL		Mgdin	9.35	+.02	+4.0	AB		FF2020n	13.07	-.11	+1.0	XC		GlobalA	35.41	+.07	+6.3	GL		SmlCapGr
.09	+.9	BL		STGvSec	7.11		+1.1	SU		FF2030n	12.99	-.14	+5	XC		OverseasA	19.59	+.04	+7.8	IL		SmallCo
.10	+.3	XC														SoGenGold n	15.85	+.55	-9.0	AU		USGovSec

Listing of Selected Seasonal Key-Date Trades in Standard and Poors 500

In order to give you a sampling of high-probability short-term seasonal trades in the stock market, I have hand picked a number of trades for you. Note the following definitions of the various column headings and statistical factors:

- *Contract year.* This is the contract year for the indicated futures contract. Although these trade histories are for the futures market in S&P 500, the same patterns and dates apply to the SPY (S&P equivalent) stock. Essentially similar patterns exist in the Dow Jones Industrials and the DIA (Diamonds) stock equivalent of the Dow Industrial Average.

- *Long or short.* This indicates either a long (buy) position or a sell (short) position in the S&P or SPY.

- *Enter.* This is the date to enter the position. The research indicates the ideal entry date. If the market was closed on this date, then entry was assumed on the close of trading the next business day.

- *Exit.* This is the date to exit the position. The research indicates the ideal exit date. If the market was closed on this date, then exit was assumed on the close of trading the next business day.

- *Stop %.* This indicates the stop loss in percent of the closing price on the date of entry. The stop loss is, as explained earlier, a "close only" or closing-basis stop.

- *P/L ratio.* This figure represents the total profits divided by the total losses. The larger the ratio is, the better the trade should be.

- *Profit/loss.* This figure shows the hypothetical profit or loss generated as a result of this trade.

- *Total.* This figure represents the cumulative or running total for this seasonal trade.

5 +1.3   BL   InTE   9.69 +.04 +2.1   IM   FF2010n 13.12 -.07 +1.4   BL   FndofAmY 25.20 -.14 +5.0   MC   MidCapSecs
3 +2.5   IL   Mgdln   9.35 +.02 +4.0   AB   FF2020n 13.07 -.11 +1.0   XC   GlobalA 35.41 +.07 +6.3   GL   SmlCapGro 1
9 +.9   BL   STGvSec 7.11   +1.1   SU   FF2030n 12.99 -.14 +.5   XC   OverseasA 19.59 +.04 +7.8   IL   SmallCo   1
                                                                         SoGenGold n15.95 .55 -9.0   AU   USGovSecs 1

FIGURE 7.2 — Seasonal Trade in March S & P Jan. 13 to Jan. 18

March—SP 500

	Enter	Exit:	Stop %:	P/L Ratio:	Trade #	
Long	1/13	1/18	2.00	4.8	103564646	
Contract	Date	Price	Date	Price		
Year	In	In	Out	Out	Profit/Loss	Total
1983	13-Jan	148.1	18-Jan	148.35	0.25	0.25
1984	13-Jan	169.15	18-Jan	169.9	0.75	1
1985	14-Jan	173.35	18-Jan	173.4	0.05	1.05
1986	13-Jan	207.4	20-Jan	208.35	0.95	2
1987	13-Jan	261.35	19-Jan	271.4	10.05	12.05
1988	13-Jan	246.25	18-Jan	252.4	6.15	18.2
1989	13-Jan	286.3	18-Jan	288.7	2.4	20.6
1990	15-Jan	339.2	18-Jan	340.85	1.65	22.25
1991	14-Jan	314.35	18-Jan	333.9	19.55	41.8
1992	13-Jan	415.8	20-Jan	417.4	1.6	43.4
1993	13-Jan	433.35	18-Jan	437.3	3.95	47.35
1994	13-Jan	473.6	18-Jan	474.4	0.8	48.15
1995	13-Jan	469.05	18-Jan	471.15	2.1	50.25
1996	15-Jan	603.2	18-Jan	610.5	7.3	57.55
1997	13-Jan	764.3	20-Jan	780.15	15.85	73.4
1998	13-Jan	959.5	20-Jan	985.2	25.7	99.1
1999	13-Jan	1239	19-Jan	1257	18	117.1
2000	13-Jan	1458.5	18-Jan	1469.5	11	128.1
2001	16-Jan	1335.5	18-Jan	1356	20.5	148.6
2002	14-Jan	1140.3	18-Jan	1129.1	-11.2	137.4
2003	13-Jan	926.4	17-Jan	903.1	-23.3	114.1
2004	13-Jan	1121.3	20-Jan	1137.5	16.2	130.3

Trades:	Winners:	Losers:	% Winners:	Daily PF:
22	20	2	90.91	1.648
Avg Prof:	Avg Loss:	% Avg Prof:	% Avg Loss:	
8.24	-17.25	1.4	-1.75	

Figure 7.2 is a very good seasonal trade in the S&P market. As you can see, it has enjoyed a high degree of accuracy at over 90 percent with an average profit of about 8.24 S&P points. While the data shown are for the S&P futures contract, note that the SPDR Trust (SPY) is the stock equivalent of this market. The move should be parallel in the SPY. Note that this is a relatively short-term trade, ideally suited to our purpose as traders. The trade enters on the long side on the close of trading January 13 trading, and exits on the close of trading January 18. As in all of the key-date seasonal trades, a stop loss needs to be employed as part of the overall strategy. Finally, remember that the indicated stop loss is a "close-only stop." This means that the market must close below the indicated stop loss which is a percentage of the entry price.

Figure 7.3 is yet another high-percentage winning trade in the S&P market. This trade has been correct over 81 percent of the time, with a large average profit per trade of over 11 S&P points. The trade enters the long side on the close of trading on February 26, and exits on the close of April 6. This trade has been a very consistent performer, but please do note that there has been one large losing year (2001). Note also that after the large losing year the trade came back strongly, recovering more than it lost the year before.

Another good trade on the long side of S&P is to buy on the close of trading March 1 and to exit on March 6 (see Figure 7.4). Although this trade is not as accurate as some of the other key-date seasonals, it does have a fairly good average profit per trade. The last two years showed losses, which generally means that the next trade will be profitable.

Figure 7.5 shows another high-probability trade in S&P is to go long on the close of trading April 14 and to exit on the close of trading April 22. This trade has shown some excellent wins with over 78 percent accuracy. The profit/loss ratio is over 9:5, which means that in total the gain was larger than the loss by nine times. The

FIGURE 7.3

Seasonal Trade in March S & P Feb. 26 to Mar. 5

March—SP 500

Long	Enter 2/26	Exit: 3/5	Stop %: 3.50	P/L Ratio: 3.9	Trade # 103593856	
Contract Year	Date In	Price In	Date Out	Price Out	Profit/Loss	Total
1983	28-Feb	149.2	7-Mar	153.6	4.4	4.4
1984	27-Feb	159.75	5-Mar	158.4	-1.35	3.05
1985	26-Feb	182.2	5-Mar	182.75	0.55	3.6
1986	26-Feb	224.65	5-Mar	225.45	0.8	4.4
1987	26-Feb	283.55	5-Mar	290.2	6.65	11.05
1988	26-Feb	263.35	7-Mar	268.3	4.95	16
1989	27-Feb	289	6-Mar	295.15	6.15	22.15
1990	26-Feb	329.85	5-Mar	334.5	4.65	26.8
1991	26-Feb	363.8	5-Mar	377.35	13.55	40.35
1992	26-Feb	415.3	5-Mar	407.4	-7.9	32.45
1993	26-Feb	443.7	5-Mar	446	2.3	34.75
1994	28-Feb	466.15	7-Mar	467.1	0.95	35.7
1995	27-Feb	484.95	6-Mar	486.2	1.25	36.95
1996	26-Feb	648.85	5-Mar	657.45	8.6	45.55
1997	26-Feb	803.75	5-Mar	804.25	0.5	46.05
1998	26-Feb	1052.1	5-Mar	1038.7	-13.4	32.65
1999	26-Feb	1235.5	5-Mar	1278.5	43	75.65
2000	28-Feb	1347.7	6-Mar	1395	47.3	122.95
2001	26-Feb	1273.6	5-Mar	1243.7	-29.9	93.05
2002	26-Feb	1107.9	5-Mar	1149.1	41.2	134.25
2003	26-Feb	827.8	5-Mar	829.5	1.7	135.95
2004	26-Feb	1143.2	5-Mar	1157.8	14.6	150.55

Trades:	Winners:	Losers:	% Winners:	Daily PF:
22	18	4	81.82	1.6119
Avg Prof:	Avg Loss:	% Avg Prof:	% Avg Loss:	
11.2833	−13.1375	1.64	−1.59	

```
.05 +1.3   BL    IntTE    9.69  +.04 +2.1   IM    FF2010n  13.12  -.07 +1.4  BL    FndotAmY  25.20  -.14 +5.0  MC    MgSecs
.03 +2.5   IL    Mgdln    9.35  +.02 +4.0   AB    FF2020n  13.07  -.11 +1.0  XC    GlobalA   35.41  +.07 +6.3  GL    SmlCapGr
.09 +.9    BL    STGvSec  7.11       +1.1   SU    FF2030n  12.99  -.14  +.5  XC    OverseasA 19.59  +.04 +7.8  IL    SmallCo
.10 +.3    XC                                                                    SoGenGold n15.85  +.55 -9.0  AU    USGovSec
```

FIGURE 7.4 ▶ Seasonal Trade in March S & P Mar. 1 to Mar. 6

March—SP 500

Contract Year	Enter 3/1 Date In	Exit: 3/6 Price In	Stop %: 1.50 Date Out	P/L Ratio: 4.1 Price Out	Trade # 103559120 Profit/Loss	Total
1983	1-Mar	152.5	7-Mar	153.6	1.1	1.1
1984	1-Mar	158.7	6-Mar	156.25	-2.45	-1.35
1985	1-Mar	183.75	6-Mar	180.85	-2.9	-4.25
1986	3-Mar	225.45	6-Mar	226.7	1.25	-3
1987	2-Mar	283.6	6-Mar	291.2	7.6	4.6
1988	1-Mar	267.65	7-Mar	268.3	0.65	5.25
1989	1-Mar	288.2	6-Mar	295.15	6.95	12.2
1990	1-Mar	333.8	6-Mar	339.2	5.4	17.6
1991	1-Mar	371.25	6-Mar	376.6	5.35	22.95
1992	2-Mar	413	6-Mar	403.9	-9.1	13.85
1993	1-Mar	442.45	8-Mar	456	13.55	27.4
1994	1-Mar	463.9	7-Mar	467.1	3.2	30.6
1995	1-Mar	486.15	6-Mar	486.2	0.05	30.65
1996	1-Mar	647.25	6-Mar	651.2	3.95	34.6
1997	3-Mar	795.25	6-Mar	800.6	5.35	39.95
1998	2-Mar	1050.1	6-Mar	1057.2	7.1	47.05
1999	1-Mar	1239	8-Mar	1283.3	44.3	91.35
2000	1-Mar	1385	6-Mar	1395	10	101.35
2001	1-Mar	1243.5	6-Mar	1257	13.5	114.85
2002	1-Mar	1132.5	6-Mar	1162.5	30	144.85
2003	3-Mar	835.4	4-Mar	822.3	-13.1	131.75
2004	1-Mar	1155.4	8-Mar	1144	-11.4	120.35

Trades:	Winners:	Losers:	% Winners:	Daily PF:
22	17	5	77.27	1.8741

Avg Prof:	Avg Loss:	% Avg Prof:	% Avg Loss:	
9.3705	−7.79	1.37	−1.57	

FIGURE 7.5 Seasonal Trade in June S & P Apr. 14 to Apr. 22

June—SP 500						
	Enter	Exit:	Stop %:	P/L Ratio:	Trade #	
Long	4/14	4/22	3.00	9.5	103745552	
Contract	Date	Price	Date	Price		
Year	In	In	Out	Out	Profit/Loss	Total
1982	21-Apr	117.45	22-Apr	117.9	0.45	0.45
1983	14-Apr	158.4	22-Apr	159.8	1.4	1.85
1984	16-Apr	160.4	23-Apr	157.95	-2.45	-0.6
1985	15-Apr	182.55	22-Apr	182.1	-0.45	-1.05
1986	14-Apr	239.05	22-Apr	242.9	3.85	2.8
1987	14-Apr	280	22-Apr	286.35	6.35	9.15
1988	14-Apr	258.4	22-Apr	261.85	3.45	12.6
1989	14-Apr	304.1	24-Apr	311.4	7.3	19.9
1990	16-Apr	346.85	20-Apr	336.4	-10.45	9.45
1991	15-Apr	382.4	22-Apr	383.3	0.9	10.35
1992	14-Apr	413.65	22-Apr	410.1	-3.55	6.8
1993	14-Apr	449.1	22-Apr	438.55	-10.55	-3.75
1994	14-Apr	445.95	22-Apr	448	2.05	-1.7
1995	17-Apr	508.4	24-Apr	515	6.6	4.9
1996	15-Apr	645.8	22-Apr	652.05	6.25	11.15
1997	14-Apr	747.3	22-Apr	780.75	33.45	44.6
1998	14-Apr	1125.1	22-Apr	1136.4	11.3	55.9
1999	14-Apr	1339.3	22-Apr	1369.1	29.8	85.7
2000	14-Apr	1367.5	24-Apr	1437	69.5	155.2
2001	16-Apr	1182	23-Apr	1226	44	199.2
2002	15-Apr	1104.3	22-Apr	1108.3	4	203.2
2003	14-Apr	886	22-Apr	909.5	23.5	226.7
2004	14-Apr	1129.7	22-Apr	1136.8	7.1	233.8

Trades:	Winners:	Losers:	% Winners:	Daily PF:
23	18	5	78.26	1.8142
Avg Prof:	Avg Loss:	% Avg Prof:	% Avg Loss:	
14.5138	-5.49	1.77	-1.59	

.05	+1.3	BL	IntTE	9.89	+.04	+2.1	IM	FF2010n	13.12	-.07	+1.4	BL	FndofAmY	25.20	-.14	+5.0	MC	MidSecS	
.03	+2.5	IL	Mgdln	9.35	+.02	+4.0	AB	FF2020n	13.07	-.11	+1.0	XC	GlobalA	35.41	+.07	+6.3	GL	SmlCapGr	
.09	+.9	BL	STGvSec	7.11		+1.1	SU	FF2030n	12.99	-.14	+.5	XC	OverseasA	19.59	+.04	+7.8	IL	SmallCo	
10	+.3	XC											SoGenGold n15.85		+.55	-9.0	AU	USGovSec	

trade has continued to grow strongly as evidenced by the cumulative profit (last column on the right).

Figure 7.6 is yet another high-odds trade for the short term, with 78 percent accuracy and a fairly large average profit per trade. By S&P standards, it has been fairly tame. Losing years have been "tolerable" in terms of their size.

Figure 7.7 is another short-term winning trade in S&P, buying on the close of trading July 10 and exiting on the close of trading July 15. While this trade has done quite well in recent years, it has not been as consistently positive a performer as I'd like to see, in spite of its fairly large accuracy and good average profit per trade.

Figure 7.8 shows buying S&P on the close of trading August 15, with an August 25 exit, has been profitable over 81 percent of the time since the start of trading in S&P futures. This trade has done quite well and has been a consistent performer as well, with over 9.00 S&P points as its average profit.

Figure 7.9 is the ultimate S&P trade! While it has shown over 95 percent accuracy, with over 154 S&P points average profit per trade, these are by no means the only two positive features that it boasts. The P/L ratio is over 200:1 with amazing winning trades since the start of trading in S&P futures. This is a fascinating trade because it tends to go long after a significant seasonal decline in stocks that preceds it. What amazes me is that although I have been teaching this trade and showing it for many years, traders always offer excuses for its not working the next time around. And yet, the trade keeps on plugging along. I'm sure that one of these years it will lose, but for the time being, it's a stellar performer.

Figure 7.10, another wonderful short-term trade, is the long on 12/20 with an exit on 1/7. This fantastic trade has averaged over 16 S&P points, with over 85 percent accuracy and some fabulous winning years. Performance has been consistent and impressive. It is likely that the trade reflects what many analysts and forecasters call the "year end rally."

FIGURE 7.6 Seasonal Trade in June S & P Jun. 1 to Jun. 6

June—SP 500							
	Enter	Exit:	Stop %:	P/L Ratio:	Trade #		
Long	6/1	6/6	2.00	6.7	103730520		
Contract	Date	Price	Date	Price			
Year	In	In	Out	Out		Profit/Loss	Total
1982	1-Jun	110.05	7-Jun	109.05		-1	-1
1983	1-Jun	162.95	6-Jun	165.45		2.5	1.5
1984	1-Jun	153.3	6-Jun	155		1.7	3.2
1985	3-Jun	190.1	6-Jun	191.65		1.55	4.75
1986	2-Jun	245.05	6-Jun	245.6		0.55	5.3
1987	1-Jun	291	8-Jun	296.35		5.35	10.65
1988	1-Jun	266.85	6-Jun	267.85		1	11.65
1989	1-Jun	322.3	6-Jun	324.85		2.55	14.2
1990	1-Jun	363.55	6-Jun	365.95		2.4	16.6
1991	3-Jun	388.35	6-Jun	384.35		-4	12.6
1992	1-Jun	416.8	8-Jun	413.6		-3.2	9.4
1993	1-Jun	453.75	7-Jun	447.65		-6.1	3.3
1994	1-Jun	457.7	6-Jun	459.35		1.65	4.95
1995	1-Jun	533.75	6-Jun	535.35		1.6	6.55
1996	3-Jun	669.45	6-Jun	673.25		3.8	10.35
1997	2-Jun	846.2	6-Jun	862.5		16.3	26.65
1998	1-Jun	1095.2	8-Jun	1117		21.8	48.45
1999	1-Jun	1295.6	7-Jun	1332.2		36.6	85.05
2000	1-Jun	1451.5	6-Jun	1463		11.5	96.55
2001	1-Jun	1265	6-Jun	1273.9		8.9	105.45
2002	3-Jun	1038.8	6-Jun	1029.5		-9.3	96.15
2003	2-Jun	968.2	6-Jun	987.8		19.6	115.75
2004	1-Jun	1121.3	7-Jun	1140.3		19	134.75

Trades:	Winners:	Losers:	% Winners:	Daily PF:
23	18	5	78.26	1.7594
Avg Prof:	Avg Loss:	% Avg Prof:	% Avg Loss:	
8.7972	-4.72	1.14	-0.98	

.05 +1.3	BL	IntTE	9.69	+.04 +2.1	IM	FF2010n	13.12	-.07 +1.4	BL	FndofAmY	25.20	-.14 +5.0	MC	MgSecs
.03 +2.5	IL	Mgdln	9.35	+.02 +4.0	AB	FF2020n	13.07	-.11 +1.0	XC	GlobalA	35.41	+.07 +6.3	GL	SmlCapGr
.09 +.9	BL	STGvSec	7.11	+1.1	SU	FF2030n	12.99	-.14 +.5	XC	OverseasA	19.59	+.04 +7.8	IL	SmallCo
.10 +.3	XC									SoGenGold n	15.85	+.55 -9.0	ALL	USGovSec

FIGURE 7.7 Seasonal Trade in September S & P Jul. 10 to Jul. 15

September—SP 500

	Enter	Exit:	Stop %:	P/L Ratio:	Trade #	
Long	7/10	7/15	1.50	5.6	88706061	
Contract	Date	Price	Date	Price		
Year	In	In	Out	Out	Profit/Loss	Total
1982	12-Jul	112.25	15-Jul	113.5	1.25	1.25
1983	11-Jul	168.9	12-Jul	166.2	-2.7	-1.45
1984	10-Jul	154.9	11-Jul	151.75	-3.15	-4.6
1985	10-Jul	194.1	15-Jul	194.05	-0.05	-4.65
1986	10-Jul	244.15	14-Jul	238.3	-5.85	-10.5
1987	10-Jul	309.45	15-Jul	312.2	2.75	-7.75
1988	11-Jul	272.45	15-Jul	272.8	0.35	-7.4
1989	10-Jul	330.5	17-Jul	335.6	5.1	-2.3
1990	10-Jul	360.5	16-Jul	372.3	11.8	9.5
1991	10-Jul	378.55	15-Jul	384.5	5.95	15.45
1992	10-Jul	415.1	15-Jul	417.2	2.1	17.55
1993	12-Jul	449.4	15-Jul	449.75	0.35	17.9
1994	11-Jul	447.2	15-Jul	454.8	7.6	25.5
1995	10-Jul	561.2	17-Jul	565.45	4.25	29.75
1996	10-Jul	661.7	11-Jul	648.35	-13.35	16.4
1997	10-Jul	921.5	15-Jul	931.75	10.25	26.65
1998	10-Jul	1172.4	15-Jul	1183.4	11	37.65
1999	12-Jul	1409.1	15-Jul	1419.4	10.3	47.95
2000	10-Jul	1491.5	17-Jul	1522	30.5	78.45
2001	10-Jul	1186.5	16-Jul	1210.5	24	102.5
2002	10-Jul	919	15-Jul	920.6	1.6	104.1
2003	10-Jul	988.7	15-Jul	1000.9	12.2	116.3

Trades:	Winners:	Losers:	% Winners:	Daily PF:
22	17	5	77.27	1.6629
Avg Prof:	Avg Loss:	% Avg Prof:	% Avg Loss:	
8.3147	−5.02	1.16	−1.61	

Seasonal Trade in September S & P Aug. 15 to Aug. 25

FIGURE 7.8

September—SP 500

	Enter	Exit:	Stop %:	P/L Ratio:	Trade #	
Long	8/15	8/25	3.50	6.4	88744323	
Contract	Date	Price	Date	Price		
Year	In	In	Out	Out	Profit/Loss	Total
1982	16-Aug	103.3	25-Aug	117.15	13.85	13.85
1983	15-Aug	164.4	25-Aug	161.55	-2.85	11
1984	15-Aug	164.65	27-Aug	167.75	3.1	14.1
1985	15-Aug	187.55	26-Aug	188.05	0.5	14.6
1986	15-Aug	248.05	25-Aug	249.6	1.55	16.15
1987	17-Aug	335.75	25-Aug	338.4	2.65	18.8
1988	15-Aug	259.1	25-Aug	259.7	0.6	19.4
1989	15-Aug	347.6	25-Aug	352.4	4.8	24.2
1990	15-Aug	341.65	17-Aug	328.65	-13	11.2
1991	15-Aug	390.95	26-Aug	394.5	3.55	14.75
1992	17-Aug	420.9	25-Aug	411.2	-9.7	5.05
1993	16-Aug	452.35	25-Aug	461.1	8.75	13.8
1994	15-Aug	462.05	25-Aug	468.4	6.35	20.15
1995	15-Aug	560.05	25-Aug	562.05	2	22.15
1996	15-Aug	663.6	26-Aug	664.2	0.6	22.75
1997	15-Aug	898.8	25-Aug	923.35	24.55	47.3
1998	17-Aug	1084.5	25-Aug	1095.5	11	58.3
1999	16-Aug	1339.4	25-Aug	1383	43.6	101.9
2000	15-Aug	1494.8	25-Aug	1513.6	18.8	120.7
2001	15-Aug	1180.8	27-Aug	1180.5	-0.3	120.4
2002	15-Aug	930.5	26-Aug	947.5	17	137.4
2003	15-Aug	990.5	25-Aug	993.7	3.2	140.6

Trades:	Winners:	Losers:	% Winners:	Daily PF:
22	18	4	81.82	0.9247
Avg Prof:	Avg Loss:	% Avg Prof:	% Avg Loss:	
9.2472	−6.4625	1.87	−1.96	

.05 +1.3 BL   IntTE   9.69 +.04 +2.1 IM   FF2010n 13.12 -.07 +1.4 BL   FndofAmY 25.20 -.14 +5.0 MC   MigSecs
.03 +2.5 IL   Mgdin   9.35 +.02 +4.0 AB   FF2020n 13.07 -.11 +1.0 XC   GlobalA   35.41 +.07 +6.3 GL   SmlCapGr
.09 +.9   BL   STGvSec 7.11   +1.1 SU   FF2030n 12.99 -.14 +.5 XC   OverseasA 19.59 +.04 +7.8 IL   SmallCo
.10 +.3   XC   SoGenGold n15.85 +.55 -.0 n ALL   USGovSec

FIGURE 7.9 Seasonal Trade in December S & P Oct. 27 to Nov. 1

December—SP 500

	Enter	Exit:	Stop %:	P/L Ratio:	Trade #	
Long	10/27	11/1	1.50	207.7	103877546	
Contract	Date	Price	Date	Price		
Year	In	In	Out	Out	Profit/Loss	Total
1982	27-Oct	135.2	1-Nov	137.45	2.25	2.25
1983	27-Oct	167.15	1-Nov	165.6	-1.55	0.7
1984	29-Oct	167.6	1-Nov	170.4	2.8	3.5
1985	28-Oct	188.1	1-Nov	191.2	3.1	6.6
1986	27-Oct	239.2	3-Nov	245.95	6.75	13.35
1987	27-Oct	228.6	2-Nov	257.75	29.15	42.5
1988	27-Oct	279.25	1-Nov	280.15	0.9	43.4
1989	27-Oct	337.2	1-Nov	343.3	6.1	49.5
1990	29-Oct	304	1-Nov	308.45	4.45	53.95
1991	28-Oct	390.6	1-Nov	391.8	1.2	55.15
1992	27-Oct	418	2-Nov	422.05	4.05	59.2
1993	27-Oct	465.7	1-Nov	469.45	3.75	62.95
1994	27-Oct	467.2	1-Nov	469.15	1.95	64.9
1995	27-Oct	583.5	1-Nov	588.25	4.75	69.65
1996	28-Oct	700.35	1-Nov	706.5	6.15	75.8
1997	27-Oct	874	3-Nov	945.7	71.7	147.5
1998	27-Oct	1074.5	2-Nov	1121.2	46.7	194.2
1999	27-Oct	1305.5	1-Nov	1362.5	57	251.2
2000	27-Oct	1401	1-Nov	1431	30	281.2
2001	29-Oct	1073	1-Nov	1082	9	290.2
2002	28-Oct	891.8	1-Nov	898.5	6.7	296.9
2003	27-Oct	1030.7	3-Nov	1054.2	23.5	320.4

Trades:	Winners:	Losers:	% Winners:	Daily PF:
22	21	1	95.45	3.0661
Avg Prof:	Avg Loss:	% Avg Prof:	% Avg Loss:	
15.3309	−1.55	2.44	−0.92	

5 +1.3   BL   IntTE   9.09 +.04 +2.1   IM   FF2010n 13.12 -.07 +1.4 BL   FndofAmY 25.20 -.14 +5.0   MC   MigSecs
3 +2.5   IL   MgdIn   9.35 +.02 +4.0   AB   FF2020n 13.07 -.11 +1.0 XC   GlobalA   35.41 +.07 +6.3   GL   SmlCapGro 1
9 +.9   BL   STGvSec   7.11   +1.1   SU   FF2030n 12.99 -.14 +.5 XC   OverseasA 19.59 +.04 +7.8   IL   SmallCo   1
                                                                                SoGenGold n15.85 +.55 -9.0   AL   USGovSecs 1

FIGURE 7.10 ▶ Seasonal Trade in March S & P Dec. 20 to Jan. 7

March—SP 500

	Enter	Exit:	Stop %:	P/L Ratio:	Trade #	
Long	12/20	1/7	3.00	10.4	103589157	
Contract	Date	Price	Date	Price		
Year	In	In	Out	Out	Profit/Loss	Total
1983	20-Dec	136.85	7-Jan	147	10.15	10.15
1984	20-Dec	165.2	9-Jan	170.8	5.6	15.75
1985	20-Dec	170.45	7-Jan	167.05	-3.4	12.35
1986	20-Dec	213.7	7-Jan	216.05	2.35	14.7
1987	22-Dec	248.8	7-Jan	256.25	7.45	22.15
1988	21-Dec	252.35	7-Jan	262.85	10.5	32.65
1989	20-Dec	281.3	9-Jan	283.7	2.4	35.05
1990	20-Dec	347.85	8-Jan	357.55	9.7	44.75
1991	20-Dec	332.85	7-Jan	317.55	-15.3	29.45
1992	20-Dec	388.35	7-Jan	419.45	31.1	60.55
1993	21-Dec	441.55	7-Jan	430.2	-11.35	49.2
1994	20-Dec	467.4	7-Jan	471.25	3.85	53.05
1995	20-Dec	460.45	9-Jan	463.75	3.3	56.35
1996	20-Dec	613.05	8-Jan	622.4	9.35	65.7
1997	20-Dec	757.25	7-Jan	759.65	2.4	68.1
1998	22-Dec	962.8	7-Jan	974	11.2	79.3
1999	21-Dec	1214.6	7-Jan	1277.8	63.2	142.5
2000	20-Dec	1435	7-Jan	1460.5	25.5	168
2001	20-Dec	1279.6	8-Jan	1309.5	29.9	197.9
2002	20-Dec	1142.3	7-Jan	1166.8	24.5	222.4
2003	20-Dec	896.7	7-Jan	923.8	27.1	249.5
2004	22-Dec	1092.7	7-Jan	1125.6	32.9	282.4

Trades:	Winners:	Losers:	% Winners:	Daily PF:
22	19	3	86.36	0.9135
Avg Prof:	Avg Loss:	% Avg Prof:	% Avg Loss:	
16.4447	−10.0166	2.77	−3.05	

▶ Key-Date Seasonals in Individual Stocks and Indices

Now that we've looked at some key-date, short-term, high-odds seasonal trades in S&P, let's look at some similar trades with longer histories in stocks (Figures 7.11 to 7.24). I show you these lest you form the erroneous conclusion that the seasonal patterns I refer to in this chapter exist only in the S&P. Now that you know how to read these historical tables, you can analyze them without my assistance.

FIGURE 7.11 Alcoa—AA, Jan. 22 to Feb. 18

Alcoa—AA							
	Enter	Exit:	Stop %:	P/L Ratio:		Trade #	
Long	1/22	2/18	15	3.3		131109668	
Entry Year	Date In	Price In	Date Out	Price Out	Profit/ Loss	P/L Pct	Total P/L
1972	24-Jan	2.77	18-Feb	2.91	0.14	5.05	0.14
1973	22-Jan	3.51	20-Feb	3.31	-0.2	-5.69	-0.06
1974	22-Jan	4.83	4-Feb	2.74	-2.09	-43.27	-2.15
1975	22-Jan	1.82	18-Feb	2.24	0.42	23.07	-1.73
1976	22-Jan	2.66	18-Feb	3.04	0.38	14.28	-1.35
1977	24-Jan	3.52	18-Feb	3.38	-0.14	-3.97	-1.49
1978	23-Jan	2.56	21-Feb	2.47	-0.09	-3.51	-1.58
1979	22-Jan	3.11	20-Feb	3.29	0.18	5.78	-1.4
1980	22-Jan	3.91	19-Feb	4.18	0.27	6.9	-1.13
1981	22-Jan	3.86	18-Feb	4.01	0.15	3.88	-0.98
1982	22-Jan	3	18-Feb	2.85	-0.15	-5	-1.13
1983	24-Jan	3.77	18-Feb	4.03	0.26	6.89	-0.87
1984	23-Jan	5.63	18-Feb	4.76	-0.87	-15.45	-1.74
1985	22-Jan	4.75	19-Feb	4.76	0.01	0.21	-1.73
1986	22-Jan	4.76	18-Feb	5.59	0.83	17.43	-0.9
1987	22-Jan	4.93	18-Feb	5.49	0.56	11.35	-0.34
1988	22-Jan	5.32	18-Feb	5.61	0.29	5.45	-0.05
1989	23-Jan	7.72	21-Feb	8.02	0.3	3.88	0.25
1990	22-Jan	7.97	20-Feb	7.75	-0.22	-2.76	0.03
1991	22-Jan	7.32	19-Feb	8.45	1.13	15.43	1.16
1992	22-Jan	8.41	18-Feb	8.81	0.4	4.75	1.56
1993	22-Jan	8.78	18-Feb	9.05	0.27	3.07	1.83
1994	24-Jan	9.45	18-Feb	9.75	0.3	3.17	2.13
1995	23-Jan	10.78	21-Feb	10.33	-0.45	-4.17	1.68
1996	22-Jan	13.06	20-Feb	13.56	0.5	3.82	2.18
1997	22-Jan	17.28	18-Feb	17.57	0.29	1.67	2.47
1998	22-Jan	16.91	18-Feb	18.63	1.72	10.17	4.19
1999	22-Jan	20.32	18-Feb	20.49	0.17	0.83	4.36
2000	24-Jan	36.72	18-Feb	37.56	0.84	2.28	5.2
2001	22-Jan	33.56	20-Feb	35.2	1.64	4.88	6.84
2002	22-Jan	33.95	19-Feb	35.25	1.3	3.82	8.14
2003	22-Jan	20.8	18-Feb	20.95	0.15	0.72	8.29
2004	22-Jan	36.43	18-Feb	37.79	1.36	3.73	9.65

Trades:	Winners:	Losers:	% Winners:	Daily PF:
33	25	8	75.76	0.0205
Avg Prof:	Avg Loss:	% Avg Prof:	% Avg Loss:	
0.5544	-0.5262	6.5	–10.48	

.05 +1.3	BL	IntTE	9.69	+.04 +2.1	IM		FF2010n	13.12	−.07 +1.4	BL		FndofAmY	25.20	−.14 +5.0	MC		MySecs
.03 +2.5	IL	Mgdin	9.35	+.02 +4.0	AB		FF2020n	13.07	−.11 +1.0	XC		GlobalA	35.41	+.07 +6.3	GL		SmlCapGr
.09 +.9	BL	STGvSec	7.11	+1.1	SU		FF2030n	12.99	−.14 +.5	XC		OverseasA	19.59	+.04 +7.8	IL		SmallCo
.10 +.3	XC											SoGenGoldn	15.85	+.55 −.9.0	ALI		USGovSec

FIGURE 7.12 Coca-Cola—KO, Mar. 31 to Jun. 6

Coca-Cola—KO

	Enter	Exit:	Stop %:	P/L Ratio:	Trade #		
Long	3/31	6/6	100	33.0	156415207		
Entry Year	Date In	Price In	Date Out	Price Out	Profit/ Loss	P/L Pct	Total P/L
1970	31-Mar	1.63	8-Jun	1.47	-0.16	-9.81	-0.16
1971	31-Mar	1.91	7-Jun	2.11	0.2	10.47	0.04
1972	3-Apr	2.55	6-Jun	2.64	0.09	3.52	0.13
1973	2-Apr	2.8	6-Jun	2.83	0.03	1.07	0.16
1974	1-Apr	2.22	6-Jun	2.31	0.09	4.05	0.25
1975	31-Mar	1.59	6-Jun	1.89	0.3	18.86	0.55
1976	31-Mar	1.78	7-Jun	1.58	-0.2	-11.23	0.35
1977	31-Mar	1.56	6-Jun	1.53	-0.03	-1.92	0.32
1978	31-Mar	1.53	6-Jun	1.78	0.25	16.33	0.57
1979	2-Apr	1.64	6-Jun	1.56	-0.08	-4.87	0.49
1980	31-Mar	1.31	6-Jun	1.42	0.11	8.39	0.6
1981	31-Mar	1.53	8-Jun	1.55	0.02	1.3	0.62
1982	31-Mar	1.36	7-Jun	1.41	0.05	3.67	0.67
1983	31-Mar	2.23	6-Jun	2.28	0.05	2.24	0.72
1984	2-Apr	2.28	6-Jun	2.36	0.08	3.5	0.8
1985	1-Apr	2.92	6-Jun	2.95	0.03	1.02	0.83
1986	31-Mar	4.39	6-Jun	4.78	0.39	8.88	1.22
1987	31-Mar	5.72	8-Jun	5.44	-0.28	-4.89	0.94
1988	31-Mar	4.78	6-Jun	4.78	0	0	0.94
1989	31-Mar	6.41	6-Jun	7.19	0.78	12.16	1.72
1990	2-Apr	9.5	6-Jun	11.34	1.84	19.36	3.56
1991	1-Apr	13.69	6-Jun	13.72	0.03	0.21	3.59
1992	31-Mar	20.44	8-Jun	21.81	1.37	6.7	4.96
1993	31-Mar	21.31	7-Jun	20.5	-0.81	-3.8	4.15
1994	31-Mar	20.31	6-Jun	21.06	0.75	3.69	4.9
1995	31-Mar	28.19	6-Jun	30.13	1.94	6.88	6.84
1996	1-Apr	42.13	6-Jun	46.75	4.62	10.96	11.46
1997	31-Mar	55.75	6-Jun	67.75	12	21.52	23.46
1998	31-Mar	77.44	8-Jun	81.06	3.62	4.67	27.08
1999	31-Mar	61.38	7-Jun	67.75	6.37	10.37	33.45
2000	31-Mar	46.94	6-Jun	51.81	4.87	10.37	38.32
2001	2-Apr	45.88	6-Jun	46.75	0.87	1.89	39.19
2002	1-Apr	52.3	6-Jun	54.15	1.85	3.53	41.04
2003	31-Mar	40.48	6-Jun	46.89	6.41	15.83	47.45
2004	31-Mar	50.3	7-Jun	52.71	2.41	4.79	49.86

Trades:	Winners:	Losers:	% Winners:	Daily PF:
35	28	7	80	0.0274
Avg Prof:	Avg Loss:	% Avg Prof:	% Avg Loss:	
1.8364	−0.2228	7.72	−5.22	

General Electric—GE, May 25 to Jun. 6

FIGURE 7.13

General Electric—GE

	Enter	Exit:	Stop %:	P/L Ratio:	Trade #		
Long	5/25	6/6	6	2.1	145913475		
Entry	Date	Price	Date	Price	Profit/	P/L	Total
Year	In	In	Out	Out	Loss	Pct	P/L
1970	25-May	0.64	8-Jun	0.7	0.06	9.37	0.06
1971	25-May	1.25	7-Jun	1.28	0.03	2.4	0.09
1972	25-May	1.45	6-Jun	1.44	-0.01	-0.68	0.08
1973	25-May	1.25	6-Jun	1.23	-0.02	-1.6	0.06
1974	28-May	1	6-Jun	1.03	0.03	3	0.09
1975	27-May	0.95	6-Jun	0.98	0.03	3.15	0.12
1976	25-May	1.05	7-Jun	1.09	0.04	3.8	0.16
1977	25-May	1.13	6-Jun	1.14	0.01	0.88	0.17
1978	25-May	1.09	6-Jun	1.13	0.04	3.66	0.21
1979	25-May	1.03	6-Jun	1.05	0.02	1.94	0.23
1980	27-May	1.03	6-Jun	1.05	0.02	1.94	0.25
1981	26-May	1.38	8-Jun	1.38	0	0	0.25
1982	25-May	1.3	7-Jun	1.27	-0.03	-2.3	0.22
1983	25-May	2.22	6-Jun	2.34	0.12	5.4	0.34
1984	25-May	2.17	6-Jun	2.22	0.05	2.3	0.39
1985	28-May	2.53	6-Jun	2.59	0.06	2.37	0.45
1986	27-May	3.36	6-Jun	3.41	0.05	1.48	0.5
1987	26-May	4.42	8-Jun	4.5	0.08	1.8	0.58
1988	25-May	3.33	6-Jun	3.56	0.23	6.9	0.81
1989	25-May	4.39	6-Jun	4.58	0.19	4.32	1
1990	25-May	5.7	6-Jun	5.78	0.08	1.4	1.08
1991	28-May	6.17	6-Jun	6.27	0.1	1.62	1.18
1992	26-May	6.27	8-Jun	6.36	0.09	1.43	1.27
1993	25-May	7.69	7-Jun	7.8	0.11	1.43	1.38
1994	25-May	7.92	6-Jun	8.13	0.21	2.65	1.59
1995	25-May	9.42	6-Jun	9.61	0.19	2.01	1.78
1996	28-May	13.8	6-Jun	14.38	0.58	4.2	2.36
1997	27-May	20.3	6-Jun	20.75	0.45	2.21	2.81
1998	26-May	27.83	8-Jun	28.14	0.31	1.11	3.12
1999	25-May	34.13	7-Jun	34.81	0.68	1.99	3.8
2000	25-May	50.75	6-Jun	51.19	0.44	0.86	4.24
2001	25-May	49.95	6-Jun	48.75	-1.2	-2.4	3.04
2002	28-May	32.05	3-Jun	30.11	-1.94	-6.05	1.1
2003	27-May	28.31	6-Jun	30.3	1.99	7.02	3.09
2004	25-May	31.21	7-Jun	31.68	0.47	1.5	3.56

Trades:	Winners:	Losers:	% Winners:	Daily PF:
35	29	6	82.86	0.0194
Avg Prof:	Avg Loss:	% Avg Prof:	% Avg Loss:	
0.2331	−0.5333	2.9	−2.17	

FIGURE 7.14 Microsoft—MSFT, Aug. 31 to Feb. 1

Microsoft—MSFT							
Long	Enter 8/31	Exit: 2/1	Stop %: 100	P/L Ratio: 10.2	Trade # 162749449		
Entry Year	Date In	Price In	Date Out	Price Out	Profit/ Loss	P/L Pct	Total P/L
1986	2-Sep	0.09	2-Feb	0.25	0.16	177.77	0.16
1987	31-Aug	0.41	1-Feb	0.38	-0.03	-7.31	0.13
1988	31-Aug	0.34	1-Feb	0.41	0.07	20.58	0.2
1989	31-Aug	0.41	1-Feb	0.65	0.24	58.53	0.44
1990	31-Aug	0.86	1-Feb	1.39	0.53	61.62	0.97
1991	3-Sep	1.73	3-Feb	2.6	0.87	50.28	1.84
1992	31-Aug	2.33	1-Feb	2.73	0.4	17.16	2.24
1993	31-Aug	2.35	1-Feb	2.66	0.31	13.19	2.55
1994	31-Aug	3.63	1-Feb	3.69	0.06	1.65	2.61
1995	31-Aug	5.78	1-Feb	5.89	0.11	1.9	2.72
1996	3-Sep	7.71	3-Feb	12.8	5.09	66.01	7.81
1997	2-Sep	17.15	2-Feb	19.36	2.21	12.88	10.02
1998	31-Aug	23.99	1-Feb	43.24	19.25	80.24	29.27
1999	31-Aug	46.28	1-Feb	51.47	5.19	11.21	34.46
2000	31-Aug	34.9	1-Feb	31.19	-3.71	-10.63	30.75
2001	31-Aug	28.52	1-Feb	31.33	2.81	9.85	33.56
2002	3-Sep	23.51	3-Feb	24.28	0.77	3.27	34.33
2003	2-Sep	27.26	2-Feb	27.4	0.14	0.51	34.47

Trades:	Winners:	Losers:	% Winners:	Daily PF:
18	16	2	88.89	0.0155
Avg Prof:	Avg Loss:	% Avg Prof:	% Avg Loss:	
2.3881	−1.87	36.67	−8.97	

FIGURE 7.15 ▶ Newmont Mining—NEM, Sep. 26 to Oct. 27

Newmont Mining—NEM

	Enter	Exit:	Stop %:	P/L Ratio:	Trade #		
Long	9/26	10/27	100	7.7	165513508		
Entry Year	Date In	Price In	Date Out	Price Out	Profit/ Loss	P/L Pct	Total P/L
1982	27-Sep	15.53	27-Oct	16.63	-1.1	-7.08	-1.1
1983	26-Sep	21.44	27-Oct	19.23	2.21	10.3	1.11
1984	26-Sep	14.31	29-Oct	14.27	0.04	0.27	1.15
1985	26-Sep	17.27	28-Oct	18.06	-0.79	-4.57	0.36
1986	26-Sep	24.03	27-Oct	23.78	0.25	1.04	0.61
1987	28-Sep	77.7	27-Oct	23.23	54.47	70.1	55.08
1988	26-Sep	27.94	27-Oct	27.44	0.5	1.78	55.58
1989	26-Sep	32.55	27-Oct	32.23	0.32	0.98	55.9
1990	26-Sep	34.55	29-Oct	28.84	5.71	16.52	61.61
1991	26-Sep	29.84	28-Oct	32.95	-3.11	-10.42	58.5
1992	28-Sep	39.05	27-Oct	35.34	3.71	9.5	62.21
1993	27-Sep	38.34	27-Oct	42.66	-4.32	-11.26	57.89
1994	26-Sep	45.75	27-Oct	40.75	40.75	10.92	62.89
1995	26-Sep	43.00	27-Oct	37.63	5.37	12.48	68.26
1996	26-Sep	47.75	28-Oct	47.25	0.5	1.04	68.76
1997	26-Sep	43.00	27-Oct	34.63	8.37	19.46	77.13
1998	28-Sep	24.75	27-Oct	0.23	1.75	7.07	78.88
1999	27-Sep	27.81	27-Oct	22.56	5.25	18.87	84.13
2000	26-Sep	16.38	27-Oct	13.69	2.69	16.42	86.82
2001	26-Sep	23.37	29-Oct	21.66	1.71	7.31	88.53
2002	26-Sep	27.25	28-Oct	25.16	2.09	7.66	90.62
2003	26-Sep	38.91	27-Oct	42.55	-3.64	-9.35	86.98

Trades:	Winners:	Losers:	% Winners:	Daily PF:
22	17	5	77.27	0.1896
Avg Prof:	Avg Loss:	% Avg Prof:	% Avg Loss:	
5.8788	-2.592	12.45	-8.54	

05 +1.3 BL   IntTE   9.69 +.04 +2.1 IM
.03 +2.5 IL   Mgdln   9.35 +.02 +4.0 AB
.09 +.9 BL   STGvSec 7.11   +1.1 SU
.10 +.3 XC

FF2010 n 13.12 −.07 +1.4 BL
FF2020 n 13.07 −.11 +1.0 XC
FF2030 n 12.99 −.14 +.5 XC

FndofAmY 25.20 −.14 +5.0 MC
GlobalA   35.41 +.07 +6.3 GL
OverseasA 19.59 +.04 +7.8 IL
SoGenGold n15.85 +.55 −9.0 ALL

SmiCapGr
SmallCo
USGovSec

FIGURE 7.16 Proctor & Gamble—PG, Oct. 26 to Dec. 27

Proctor & Gamble—PG

Long	Enter 10/26	Exit: 12/27	Stop %: 100	P/L Ratio: 54.9	Trade # 170642713		
Entry Year	Date In	Price In	Date Out	Price Out	Profit/ Loss	P/L Pct	Total P/L
1970	26-Oct	1.67	28-Dec	1.79	0.12	7.18	0.12
1971	26-Oct	2.18	27-Dec	2.4	0.22	10.09	0.34
1972	26-Oct	3.11	27-Dec	3.42	0.31	9.96	0.65
1973	26-Oct	3.3	27-Dec	2.88	-0.42	-12.72	0.23
1974	28-Oct	2.61	27-Dec	2.49	-0.12	-4.59	0.11
1975	27-Oct	2.78	29-Dec	2.8	0.02	0.71	0.13
1976	26-Oct	2.85	27-Dec	2.87	0.02	0.7	0.15
1977	26-Oct	2.58	27-Dec	2.65	0.07	2.71	0.22
1978	26-Oct	2.63	27-Dec	2.77	0.14	5.32	0.36
1979	26-Oct	2.32	27-Dec	2.33	0.01	0.43	0.37
1980	27-Oct	2.19	29-Dec	2.14	-0.05	-2.28	0.32
1981	26-Oct	2.31	28-Dec	2.49	0.18	7.79	0.5
1982	26-Oct	3.45	27-Dec	3.82	0.37	10.72	0.87
1983	26-Oct	3.61	27-Dec	3.6	-0.01	-0.27	0.86
1984	26-Oct	3.57	27-Dec	3.56	-0.01	-0.28	0.85
1985	28-Oct	3.88	27-Dec	4.35	0.47	12.11	1.32
1986	27-Oct	4.6	29-Dec	4.89	0.29	6.3	1.61
1987	26-Oct	4.97	28-Dec	5.33	0.36	7.24	1.97
1988	26-Oct	5.2	27-Dec	5.38	0.18	3.46	2.15
1989	26-Oct	7.92	27-Dec	8.5	0.58	7.32	2.73
1990	26-Oct	9.7	27-Dec	10.75	1.05	10.82	3.78
1991	28-Oct	10.39	27-Dec	11.3	0.91	8.75	4.69
1992	26-Oct	13.38	28-Dec	13.72	0.34	2.54	5.03
1993	26-Oct	13.03	27-Dec	14.56	1.53	11.74	6.56
1994	26-Oct	15.56	27-Dec	15.78	0.22	1.41	6.78
1995	26-Oct	20.47	27-Dec	20.78	0.31	1.51	7.09
1996	28-Oct	23.82	27-Dec	27.5	3.68	15.44	10.77
1997	27-Oct	32.85	29-Dec	39.9	7.05	21.46	17.82
1998	26-Oct	43.81	28-Dec	46.56	2.75	6.27	20.57
1999	26-Oct	49.1	27-Dec	55.63	6.53	13.29	27.1
2000	26-Oct	37.47	27-Dec	38.25	0.78	2.08	27.88
2001	26-Oct	36.67	27-Dec	40.08	3.41	9.29	31.29
2002	28-Oct	42.88	27-Dec	43.28	0.4	0.93	31.69
2003	27-Oct	48.4	29-Dec	49.6	1.2	2.47	32.89

Trades: 34	Winners: 29	Losers: 5	% Winners: 85.29	Daily PF: 0.0186
Avg Prof: 1.1551	Avg Loss: −0.122	% Avg Prof: 6.9	% Avg Loss: −4.03	

FIGURE 7.17 ▸ Sun Microsystems—SUNW, Nov. 2 to Jan. 18

Sun Microsystems—SUNW							
	Enter	Exit:	Stop %:	P/L Ratio:	Trade #		
Long	11/2	1/18	100	1.3	173009506		
Entry Year	Date In	Price In	Date Out	Price Out	Profit/ Loss	P/L Pct	Total P/L
1987	2-Nov	0.53	18-Jan	0.56	0.03	5.66	0.03
1988	2-Nov	0.45	18-Jan	0.55	0.1	22.22	0.13
1989	2-Nov	0.51	18-Jan	0.53	0.02	3.92	0.15
1990	2-Nov	0.53	18-Jan	0.85	0.32	60.37	0.47
1991	4-Nov	0.72	20-Jan	1.03	0.31	43.05	0.78
1992	2-Nov	1.05	18-Jan	1.15	0.1	9.52	0.88
1993	2-Nov	0.79	18-Jan	0.88	0.09	11.39	0.97
1994	2-Nov	1.03	18-Jan	1.08	0.05	4.85	1.02
1995	2-Nov	2.47	18-Jan	2.79	0.32	12.95	1.34
1996	4-Nov	3.87	20-Jan	4.05	0.18	4.65	1.52
1997	3-Nov	4.58	20-Jan	5.9	1.32	28.82	2.84
1998	2-Nov	7.27	19-Jan	13.16	5.89	81.01	8.73
1999	2-Nov	25.92	18-Jan	40.38	14.46	55.78	23.19
2000	2-Nov	54.53	18-Jan	34.88	-19.65	-36.03	3.54
2001	2-Nov	11.44	18-Jan	12.12	0.68	5.94	4.22
2002	4-Nov	3.2	21-Jan	3.55	0.35	10.93	4.57
2003	3-Nov	4.39	20-Jan	5.59	1.2	27.33	5.77

Trades:	Winners:	Losers:	% Winners:	Daily PF:
17	16	1	94.12	0.0206
Avg Prof:	Avg Loss:	% Avg Prof:	% Avg Loss:	
1.5887	-19.65	24.27	-36.03	

FIGURE 7.18 ▶ Texas Instruments—TXN, Dec. 15 to Apr. 19

Texas Instruments—TXN

| | Enter | Exit: | Stop %: | P/L Ratio: | Trade # | | |
| Long | 12/15 | 4/19 | 100 | 5.7 | 175382055 | | |
Entry Year	Date In	Price In	Date Out	Price Out	Profit/ Loss	P/L Pct	Total P/L
1970	15-Dec	0.83	19-Apr	1.09	0.26	31.32	0.26
1971	15-Dec	1.25	19-Apr	1.52	0.27	21.6	0.53
1972	15-Dec	1.8	19-Apr	1.86	0.06	3.33	0.59
1973	17-Dec	1.97	19-Apr	2.08	0.11	5.58	0.7
1974	16-Dec	1.38	21-Apr	2.2	0.82	59.42	1.52
1975	15-Dec	1.94	19-Apr	2.5	0.56	28.86	2.08
1976	15-Dec	2.09	19-Apr	1.78	-0.31	-14.83	1.77
1977	15-Dec	1.52	19-Apr	1.53	0.01	0.65	1.78
1978	15-Dec	1.61	19-Apr	1.7	0.09	5.59	1.87
1979	17-Dec	1.89	21-Apr	1.69	-0.2	-10.58	1.67
1980	15-Dec	2.63	20-Apr	2.53	-0.1	-3.8	1.57
1981	15-Dec	1.64	19-Apr	1.86	0.22	13.41	1.79
1982	15-Dec	2.69	19-Apr	3.33	0.64	23.79	2.43
1983	15-Dec	2.83	19-Apr	2.89	0.06	2.12	2.49
1984	17-Dec	2.36	19-Apr	1.94	-0.42	-17.79	2.07
1985	16-Dec	2.23	21-Apr	2.84	0.61	27.35	2.68
1986	15-Dec	2.56	20-Apr	4.02	1.46	57.03	4.14
1987	15-Dec	0.03	19-Apr	3.14	0.14	4.66	4.28
1988	15-Dec	2.44	19-Apr	2.59	0.15	6.14	4.43
1989	15-Dec	2.19	19-Apr	2.22	0.03	1.36	4.46
1990	17-Dec	2.19	19-Apr	2.66	0.47	21.46	4.93
1991	16-Dec	1.73	20-Apr	2.22	0.49	28.32	5.42
1992	15-Dec	2.88	19-Apr	3.34	0.46	15.97	5.88
1993	15-Dec	3.88	19-Apr	4.16	0.28	7.21	6.16
1994	15-Dec	4.59	19-Apr	5.75	1.16	25.27	7.32
1995	15-Dec	6.13	19-Apr	6.89	0.76	12.39	8.08
1996	16-Dec	7.8	21-Apr	10.36	2.56	32.82	10.64
1997	15-Dec	10.63	20-Apr	15.31	4.68	44.02	15.32
1998	15-Dec	19.59	19-Apr	26.25	6.66	33.99	21.98
1999	15-Dec	47.69	19-Apr	71.5	23.81	49.92	45.79
2000	15-Dec	0.47	19-Apr	38.81	-8.19	-17.42	37.6
2001	17-Dec	30.17	19-Apr	33.3	3.13	10.37	40.73
2002	16-Dec	17.25	21-Apr	19.37	2.12	12.28	42.85
2003	15-Dec	28.34	19-Apr	28.4	0.06	0.21	42.91

Trades:	Winners:	Losers:	% Winners:	Daily PF:
34	29	5	85.29	0.0143
Avg Prof:	Avg Loss:	% Avg Prof:	% Avg Loss:	
1.7975	−1.844	20.22	−12.88	

FIGURE
7.19

Long DJ Industrial Average, Nov. 17 to Jan. 4

Long DJ Industrial Average							
	Enter	Exit:	Stop %:	P/L Ratio:			
	11/17	1/4	9	219.5			
Entry Year	Date In	Price In	Date Out	Price Out	Profit/ Loss	P/L Pct	Total P/L
1970	17-Nov	760.5	4-Jan	830.6	70.1	9.21	70.1
1971	17-Nov	822.1	4-Jan	892.2	70.1	8.52	140.2
1972	17-Nov	1005.6	4-Jan	1039.8	34.2	3.4	174.4
1973	19-Nov	862.7	4-Jan	880.2	17.5	2.02	191.9
1974	18-Nov	624.9	6-Jan	637.2	12.3	1.96	204.2
1975	17-Nov	856.7	5-Jan	877.8	21.1	2.46	225.3
1976	17-Nov	938.1	4-Jan	987.9	49.8	5.3	275.1
1977	17-Nov	831.9	4-Jan	813.6	-18.3	-2.19	256.8
1978	17-Nov	797.7	4-Jan	826.1	28.4	3.56	285.2
1979	19-Nov	815.3	4-Jan	828.8	13.5	1.65	298.7
1980	17-Nov	986.3	5-Jan	992.7	6.4	0.64	305.1
1981	17-Nov	850.2	4-Jan	882.5	32.3	3.79	337.4
1982	17-Nov	1027.5	4-Jan	1046.1	18.6	1.81	356
1983	17-Nov	1254.7	4-Jan	1269.1	14.4	1.14	370.4
1984	19-Nov	1185.3	4-Jan	1184.9	-0.4	-0.03	370
1985	18-Nov	1440	6-Jan	1547.6	107.6	7.47	477.6
1986	17-Nov	1860.5	5-Jan	1971.3	110.8	5.95	588.4
1987	17-Nov	1922.3	4-Jan	2015.3	93	4.83	681.4
1988	17-Nov	2052.5	4-Jan	2177.7	125.2	6.09	806.6
1989	17-Nov	2652.7	4-Jan	2796.1	143.4	5.4	950
1990	19-Nov	2565.4	4-Jan	2566.1	0.7	0.02	950.7
1991	18-Nov	2972.7	6-Jan	3200.1	227.4	7.64	1178.1
1992	17-Nov	3193.3	4-Jan	3309.2	115.9	3.62	1294
1993	17-Nov	3704.4	4-Jan	3783.9	79.5	2.14	1373.5
1994	17-Nov	3828	4-Jan	3857.6	29.6	0.77	1403.1
1995	17-Nov	4990	4-Jan	5173.8	183.8	3.68	1586.9
1996	18-Nov	6346.9	6-Jan	6567.2	220.3	3.47	1807.2
1997	17-Nov	7698.2	5-Jan	7979	280.8	3.64	2088
1998	17-Nov	8986.3	4-Jan	9184.3	198	2.2	2286
1999	17-Nov	10883	4-Jan	10997.9	114.8	1.05	2400.8
2000	17-Nov	10630	4-Jan	10912.4	282.5	2.65	2683.3
2001	19-Nov	9976.5	4-Jan	10259.7	283.2	2.83	2966.5
2002	18-Nov	8486.6	6-Jan	8773.6	287	3.38	3253.5
2003	17-Nov	9710.8	5-Jan	10544.1	833.27	8.58	4086.77

Trades:	Winners:	Losers:	% Winners:	Daily PF:
34	32	2	94.12	2.6728
Avg Prof:	Avg Loss:	% Avg Prof:	% Avg Loss:	
128.2959	-9.35	3.78	-1.11	

FIGURE
7.20

Long DJ Industrial Average, Dec. 3 to Jan. 6

Long DJ Industrial Average							
	Enter 12/3	Exit: 1/6	Stop %: 9	P/L Ratio: 13.9			
Entry Year	Date In	Price In	Date Out	Price Out	Profit/ Loss	P/L Pct	Total P/L
1970	3-Dec	808.5	6-Jan	838	29.5	3.64	29.5
1971	3-Dec	859.6	6-Jan	908.5	48.9	5.68	78.4
1972	4-Dec	1027	8-Jan	1047.9	20.9	2.03	99.3
1973	3-Dec	806.5	7-Jan	876.9	70.4	8.72	169.7
1974	3-Dec	596.6	6-Jan	637.2	40.6	6.8	210.3
1975	3-Dec	825.5	6-Jan	890.8	65.3	7.91	275.6
1976	3-Dec	950.6	6-Jan	979.9	29.3	3.08	304.9
1977	5-Dec	821	6-Jan	793.5	-27.5	-3.34	277.4
1978	4-Dec	806.8	8-Jan	828.1	21.3	2.64	298.7
1979	3-Dec	819.6	7-Jan	832	12.4	1.51	311.1
1980	3-Dec	972.3	6-Jan	1004.7	32.4	3.33	343.5
1981	3-Dec	883.8	6-Jan	861	-22.8	-2.57	320.7
1982	3-Dec	1031.4	6-Jan	1070.9	39.5	3.82	360.2
1983	5-Dec	1270.5	6-Jan	1286.6	16.1	1.26	376.3
1984	3-Dec	1182.4	7-Jan	1190.6	8.2	0.69	384.5
1985	3-Dec	1459.1	6-Jan	1547.6	88.5	6.06	473
1986	3-Dec	1947.3	6-Jan	1974.8	27.5	1.41	500.5
1987	3-Dec	1776.5	6-Jan	2037.8	261.3	14.7	761.8
1988	5-Dec	2123.8	6-Jan	2194.3	70.5	3.31	832.3
1989	4-Dec	2753.6	8-Jan	2794.4	40.8	1.48	873.1
1990	3-Dec	2565.6	7-Jan	2522.8	-42.8	-1.66	830.3
1991	3-Dec	2929.6	6-Jan	3200.1	270.5	9.23	1100.8
1992	3-Dec	3276.5	6-Jan	3305.2	28.7	0.87	1129.5
1993	3-Dec	3704.1	6-Jan	3803.9	99.8	2.69	1229.3
1994	5-Dec	3741.9	6-Jan	3867.4	125.5	3.35	1354.8
1995	4-Dec	5139.5	8-Jan	5197.7	58.2	1.13	1413
1996	3-Dec	6442.7	6-Jan	6567.2	124.5	1.93	1537.5
1997	3-Dec	8032	6-Jan	7906.3	-125.7	-1.56	1411.8
1998	3-Dec	8879.7	6-Jan	9545	665.3	7.49	2077.1
1999	3-Dec	11286	6-Jan	11253.3	-32.9	-0.29	2044.2
2000	4-Dec	10560	8-Jan	10621.4	61.3	0.58	2105.5
2001	3-Dec	9764	7-Jan	10197.1	433.1	4.43	2538.6
2002	3-Dec	8742.9	6-Jan	8773.6	30.7	0.35	2569.3
2003	3-Dec	9873.4	6-Jan	10538.7	665.28	6.73	3234.58

Trades: 34	Winners: 29	Losers: 5	% Winners: 85.29	Daily PF: 3.5357
Avg Prof: 120.2165	Avg Loss: −50.34	% Avg Prof: 4.03	% Avg Loss: −1.88	

FIGURE 7.21 Long DJ Industrial Average, Feb. 18 to May 4

Long DJ Industrial Average							
	Enter	Exit:	Stop %:	P/L Ratio:			
	2/18	5/4	15	7.2			
Entry	Date	Price	Date	Price	Profit/	P/L	Total
Year	In	In	Out	Out	Loss	Pct	P/L
1970	18-Feb	756.8	4-May	714.6	-42.2	-5.57	-42.2
1971	18-Feb	885.1	4-May	938.5	53.4	6.03	11.2
1972	18-Feb	917.5	4-May	937.3	19.8	2.15	31
1973	20-Feb	983.6	4-May	953.9	-29.7	-3.01	1.3
1974	19-Feb	819.5	6-May	844.9	25.4	3.09	26.7
1975	18-Feb	731.3	5-May	855.6	124.3	16.99	151
1976	18-Feb	960.1	4-May	993.7	33.6	3.49	184.6
1977	18-Feb	940.2	4-May	940.7	0.5	0.05	185.1
1978	21-Feb	749.3	4-May	824.4	75.1	10.02	260.2
1979	20-Feb	834.5	4-May	847.5	13	1.55	273.2
1980	19-Feb	876	5-May	816.3	-59.7	-6.81	213.5
1981	18-Feb	947.1	4-May	979.1	32	3.37	245.5
1982	18-Feb	829	4-May	854.4	25.4	3.06	270.9
1983	18-Feb	1092.8	4-May	1212.7	119.9	10.97	390.8
1984	21-Feb	1139.3	4-May	1165.3	26	2.28	416.8
1985	19-Feb	1280.6	6-May	1247.8	-32.8	-2.56	384
1986	18-Feb	1678.8	5-May	1793.8	115	6.85	499
1987	18-Feb	2237.6	4-May	2286.2	48.6	2.17	547.6
1988	18-Feb	1986.4	4-May	2036.3	49.9	2.51	597.5
1989	21-Feb	2326.4	4-May	2384.9	58.5	2.51	656
1990	20-Feb	2596.9	4-May	2710.4	113.5	4.37	769.5
1991	19-Feb	2932.2	6-May	2941.6	9.4	0.32	778.9
1992	18-Feb	3224.7	4-May	3378.1	153.4	4.75	932.3
1993	18-Feb	3302.2	4-May	3446.2	144	4.36	1076.3
1994	18-Feb	3887.2	4-May	3697.8	-189.4	-4.87	886.9
1995	21-Feb	3964	4-May	4359.7	395.7	9.98	1282.6
1996	20-Feb	5458.5	6-May	5464.3	5.8	0.1	1288.4
1997	18-Feb	7067.5	5-May	7214.5	147	2.07	1435.4
1998	18-Feb	8451.1	4-May	9192.7	741.6	8.77	2177
1999	18-Feb	9298.6	4-May	10886.1	1587.5	17.07	3764.5
2000	18-Feb	10220	4-May	10412.5	193	1.88	3957.5
2001	20-Feb	10731	4-May	10951.2	220.3	2.05	4177.8
2002	19-Feb	9745.1	6-May	9808	62.9	0.64	4240.7
2003	18-Feb	8041.1	5-May	8531.6	490.5	6.09	4731.2
2004	18-Feb	10672	4-May	10317.2	-354.8	-3.32	4376.4

Trades:	Winners:	Losers:	% Winners:	Daily PF:
35	29	6	82.86	2.3379
Avg Prof:	Avg Loss:	% Avg Prof:	% Avg Loss:	
175.3448	-118.1	4.81	-4.36	

FIGURE 7.22 Long DJ Industrial Average, Mar. 13 to Mar. 18

Long DJ Industrial Average

	Enter 3/13	Exit: 3/18	Stop %: 3	P/L Ratio: 4.7			
Entry Year	Date In	Price In	Date Out	Price Out	Profit/ Loss	P/L Pct	Total P/L
1970	13-Mar	772.1	18-Mar	768	-4.1	-0.53	-4.1
1971	15-Mar	908.2	18-Mar	916.8	8.6	0.94	4.5
1972	13-Mar	928.7	20-Mar	941.2	12.5	1.34	17
1973	13-Mar	976.1	19-Mar	952.1	-24	-2.45	-7
1974	13-Mar	891.9	18-Mar	874.2	-17.7	-1.98	-24.7
1975	13-Mar	763	18-Mar	779.4	16.4	2.14	-8.3
1976	15-Mar	974.5	18-Mar	979.9	5.4	0.55	-2.9
1977	14-Mar	958.4	18-Mar	961	2.6	0.27	-0.3
1978	13-Mar	760	20-Mar	773.8	13.8	1.81	13.5
1979	13-Mar	846.9	19-Mar	857.6	10.7	1.26	24.2
1980	13-Mar	809.6	18-Mar	801.6	-8	-0.98	16.2
1981	13-Mar	985.8	18-Mar	994.1	8.3	0.84	24.5
1982	15-Mar	801	18-Mar	805.3	4.3	0.53	28.8
1983	14-Mar	1114.4	18-Mar	1117.7	3.3	0.29	32.1
1984	13-Mar	1164.8	19-Mar	1171.4	6.6	0.56	38.7
1985	13-Mar	1261.7	18-Mar	1249.7	-12	-0.95	26.7
1986	13-Mar	1753.7	18-Mar	1789.9	36.2	2.06	62.9
1987	13-Mar	2258.7	18-Mar	2286.9	28.2	1.24	91.1
1988	14-Mar	2050.1	18-Mar	2087.4	37.3	1.81	128.4
1989	13-Mar	2306.3	20-Mar	2262.5	-43.8	-1.89	84.6
1990	13-Mar	2674.6	19-Mar	2755.6	81	3.02	165.6
1991	13-Mar	2955.2	18-Mar	2929.9	-25.3	-0.85	140.3
1992	13-Mar	3235.9	18-Mar	3254.2	18.3	0.56	158.6
1993	15-Mar	3442.4	18-Mar	3465.6	23.2	0.67	181.8
1994	14-Mar	3863	18-Mar	3894.8	31.8	0.82	213.6
1995	13-Mar	4025.2	20-Mar	4083.7	58.5	1.45	272.1
1996	13-Mar	5568.7	18-Mar	5683.6	114.9	2.06	387
1997	13-Mar	6878.9	18-Mar	6896.6	17.7	0.25	404.7
1998	13-Mar	8602.5	18-Mar	8775.4	172.9	2	577.6
1999	15-Mar	9958.8	18-Mar	9997.6	38.8	0.38	616.4
2000	13-Mar	9947.1	20-Mar	10680.2	733.1	7.36	1349.5
2001	13-Mar	10291	14-Mar	9973.5	-317.3	-3.08	1032.2
2002	13-Mar	10502	18-Mar	10577.8	75.9	0.72	1108.1
2003	13-Mar	7821.8	18-Mar	8194.2	372.4	4.76	1480.5
2004	15-Mar	10103	18-Mar	10295.8	192.9	1.9	1673.4

Trades:	Winners:	Losers:	% Winners:	Daily PF:
35	27	8	77.14	15.7451
Avg Prof:	Avg Loss:	% Avg Prof:	% Avg Loss:	
78.7259	−56.525	1.54	−1.59	

FIGURE 7.23 ▶ Long DJ Industrial Average, Apr. 7 to Apr. 16

Long DJ Industrial Average

	Enter 4/7	Exit: 4/16	Stop %: 15	P/L Ratio: 2.2			
Entry Year	Date In	Price In	Date Out	Price Out	Profit/ Loss	P/L Pct	Total P/L
1970	7-Apr	791.6	16-Apr	775.9	-15.7	-1.98	-15.7
1971	7-Apr	918.5	16-Apr	940.2	21.7	2.36	6
1972	7-Apr	962.6	17-Apr	966.6	4	0.41	10
1973	9-Apr	947.6	16-Apr	956.7	9.1	0.96	19.1
1974	8-Apr	840	16-Apr	861.2	21.2	2.52	40.3
1975	7-Apr	742.9	16-Apr	815.7	72.8	9.79	113.1
1976	7-Apr	986.2	19-Apr	988.1	1.9	0.19	115
1977	7-Apr	918.9	18-Apr	942.8	23.9	2.6	138.9
1978	7-Apr	769.6	17-Apr	810.1	40.5	5.26	179.4
1979	9-Apr	873.7	16-Apr	860.4	-13.3	-1.52	166.1
1980	7-Apr	768.3	16-Apr	771.3	3	0.39	169.1
1981	7-Apr	992.9	16-Apr	1005.6	12.7	1.27	181.8
1982	7-Apr	836.9	16-Apr	843.4	6.5	0.77	188.3
1983	7-Apr	1117.7	18-Apr	1183.2	65.5	5.86	253.8
1984	9-Apr	1133.9	16-Apr	1160.4	26.5	2.33	280.3
1985	8-Apr	1253	16-Apr	1269.5	16.5	1.31	296.8
1986	7-Apr	1735.5	16-Apr	1848	112.5	6.48	409.3
1987	7-Apr	2360.9	16-Apr	2276	-84.9	-3.59	324.4
1988	7-Apr	2062.2	18-Apr	2008.1	-54.1	-2.62	270.3
1989	7-Apr	2304.8	17-Apr	2337.8	33	1.43	303.3
1990	9-Apr	2722.1	16-Apr	2763.1	41	1.5	344.3
1991	8-Apr	2918.6	16-Apr	2986.9	68.3	2.34	412.6
1992	7-Apr	3213.6	16-Apr	3366.5	152.9	4.75	565.5
1993	7-Apr	3397	16-Apr	3478.6	81.6	2.4	647.1
1994	7-Apr	3693.3	18-Apr	3620.4	-72.9	-1.97	574.2
1995	7-Apr	4192.6	17-Apr	4195.4	2.8	0.06	577
1996	8-Apr	5594.4	16-Apr	5620	25.6	0.45	602.6
1997	7-Apr	6555.9	16-Apr	6679.9	124	1.89	726.6
1998	7-Apr	8956.5	16-Apr	9076.6	120.1	1.34	846.7
1999	7-Apr	10085	16-Apr	10498.9	413.6	4.1	1260.3
2000	7-Apr	11112	17-Apr	10582.5	-529	-4.76	731.3
2001	9-Apr	9845.2	16-Apr	10158.6	313.4	3.18	1044.7
2002	8-Apr	10249	16-Apr	10301.3	52.2	0.5	1096.9
2003	7-Apr	8300.4	16-Apr	8257.6	-42.8	-0.51	1054.1
2004	7-Apr	10480	16-Apr	10452	-28.2	-0.26	1025.9

Trades: 35	Winners: 27	Losers: 8	% Winners: 77.14	Daily PF: 7.6823
Avg Prof: 69.1407	Avg Loss: -105.113	% Avg Prof: 2.46	% Avg Loss: -2.15	

Long DJ Industrial Average, May 28 to Jun. 6

FIGURE 7.24

Long DJ Industrial Average

	Enter 5/28	Exit: 6/6	Stop %: 100	P/L Ratio: 3.7			
Entry Year	Date In	Price In	Date Out	Price Out	Profit/ Loss	P/L Pct	Total P/L
1970	28-May	684.2	8-Jun	700.2	16	2.33	16
1971	28-May	907.8	7-Jun	923.1	15.3	1.68	31.3
1972	30-May	971.2	6-Jun	951.5	-19.7	-2.02	11.6
1973	29-May	925.6	6-Jun	898.2	-27.4	-2.96	-15.8
1974	28-May	814.3	6-Jun	845.4	31.1	3.81	15.3
1975	28-May	817	6-Jun	839.6	22.6	2.76	37.9
1976	28-May	975.2	7-Jun	958.1	-17.1	-1.75	20.8
1977	31-May	898.7	6-Jun	903.1	4.4	0.48	25.2
1978	30-May	831.7	6-Jun	866.5	34.8	4.18	60
1979	29-May	832.6	6-Jun	835.5	2.9	0.34	62.9
1980	28-May	860.3	6-Jun	861.5	1.2	0.13	64.1
1981	28-May	994.3	6-Jun	995.6	1.3	0.13	65.4
1982	28-May	819.5	7-Jun	804	-15.5	-1.89	49.9
1983	31-May	1200	6-Jun	1214.2	14.2	1.18	64.1
1984	29-May	1101.2	6-Jun	1133.8	32.6	2.96	96.7
1985	28-May	1301.5	6-Jun	1327.3	25.8	1.98	122.5
1986	28-May	1878.3	6-Jun	1885.9	7.6	0.4	130.1
1987	28-May	2310.7	8-Jun	2351.6	40.9	1.77	171
1988	31-May	2031.1	6-Jun	2075.2	44.1	2.17	215.1
1989	30-May	2475.6	6-Jun	2496.3	20.7	0.83	235.8
1990	29-May	2870.5	6-Jun	2911.6	41.1	1.43	276.9
1991	28-May	2958.9	6-Jun	2994.9	36	1.21	312.9
1992	28-May	3398.4	8-Jun	3404.1	5.7	0.16	318.6
1993	28-May	3527.4	7-Jun	3532.1	4.7	0.13	323.3
1994	31-May	3758.4	6-Jun	3768.5	10.1	0.26	333.4
1995	30-May	4378.7	6-Jun	4485.5	106.8	2.43	440.2
1996	28-May	5709.7	6-Jun	5667.2	-42.5	-0.74	397.7
1997	28-May	7357.2	6-Jun	7435.8	78.6	1.06	476.3
1998	28-May	8970.2	8-Jun	9069.6	99.4	1.1	575.7
1999	28-May	10557	7-Jun	10903.8	346.4	3.28	922.1
2000	30-May	10527	6-Jun	10735.6	208.5	1.98	1130.6
2001	29-May	11039	6-Jun	11070.2	31.1	0.28	1161.7
2002	28-May	9981.6	6-Jun	9624.6	-357	-3.57	804.7
2003	28-May	8793.1	6-Jun	9062.79	269.67	3.06	1074.37
2004	28-May	10189	7-Jun	10391.1	202.6	1.98	1276.97

Trades: 35	Winners: 29	Losers: 6	% Winners: 82.86	Daily PF: 6.7286
Avg Prof: 60.5575	Avg Loss: -79.8666	% Avg Prof: 1.57	% Avg Loss: -2.16	

▶ Why Are Seasonal Trades So Difficult to Follow?

During the years that I have been trading and researching key-date seasonals (as well as other types of seasonal price patterns), I have been asked many times why traders have such a difficult time following even the most historically reliable seasonal trades. It seems that with the historical accuracy of seasonals being relatively high compared to other methods of trade selection, that traders would be more inclined to use seasonals in their work. But this is apparently not the case. The question is valid and deserves thought as well as a cogent response. Given my over three decades of experience in futures and stocks, here are some thoughts that come to mind.

- A number of negative publicity campaigns have been directed at seasonals. Most of the critiques of seasonality are either misguided or based on a faulty understanding of what seasonals are and/or what they are designed to do. Anyone who takes the time and effort to study seasonality will reach the conclusion that there are some highly valid concepts and methods which derive from seasonality.

- Many traders feel that seasonals are too "obvious" and that they must therefore not be valid. Traders often wallow in the mistaken belief that in order for a system, method, or indicator to be profitable it must be complex, intricate, or mystical. I do not believe any of that! Rather, I feel that systems, methods, or indicators tend to work better if they are based on simple and basic concepts.

- Too many traders do not understand seasonality. They believe that seasonality is a direct function of weather. Yet, no matter how hard we try to explain to them that seasonals are not entirely a function of weather, they fail to understand. Certainly if traders believe that weather is the only factor that can cause a seasonal pattern to work, they will be disinclined to take action if they do not see clear-cut weather patterns.

.05 +1.3	BL	IntTE	9.69	+.04 +2.1	IM	FF2010 n	13.12	−.07 +1.4	BL	FndofAmY	25.20	−.14 +5.0	MC
.03 +2.5	IL	Mgdln	9.35	+.02 +4.0	AB	FF2020 n	13.07	−.11 +1.0	XC	GlobalA	35.41	+.07 +6.3	GL	SmlCapGr
.09 +.9	BL	STGvSec	7.11	+1.1	SU	FF2000 n	12.99	−.14 +.5	XC	OverseasA	19.59	+.04 +7.8	IL	SmallCo

- Many traders do not believe that markets such as T-Bonds, S&P, and the currencies can exhibit seasonal patterns. This erroneous belief relates to my previous point, because the seasonals in these markets are not a function of weather. Rather, they are based on other fundamental aspects of market behavior.

- Perhaps the most valid of all conclusions with regard to the question I raised above is that traders are simply a generally undisciplined lot. Whether they are asked to follow a system, method, indicator, trading program, or seasonals, the fact remains that many traders cannot carry through to completion. They are unable to follow any system. And in this respect, their inability to follow seasonals comes as no surprise. It is the inherent weakness of all traders. Very few traders can trade with the discipline that's required for success. Seasonality becomes just another tool that traders will either follow or not follow, depending on their whims. And herein, I believe, is the major reason that seasonals are so difficult for most traders to follow.

▶ The Philosophy and Psychology of Seasonals

As I close this chapter, please review the following facts and considerations with regard to seasonal trading.

It is impossible to trade stocks or futures for too long without realizing that psychology and philosophy are as much a part of the game as are systems, methods, and indicators. In fact, I'd venture to say that the philosophy and psychology of the markets are probably more important than anyone has ever dared to admit. If you're not convinced that you, as a trader, are affected by your philosophical point of view and by your psychology, then you are living in a fool's paradise! I might even go so far as to suggest that we are all slaves to our emotions and perceptions. The fact of the matter is that virtually everything you do is colored, to varying degrees, by your point of view. And your point of view is a function of how you were raised, what you believe, what you do, where you grew up, what schools you went to, childhood traumas you may have experienced, how you were disciplined as a child, who you know, how you think, your wishes, hopes, desires, dreams, and day-to-day conflicts.

Within the constraints of a few paragraphs I cannot begin to do justice to this vast and important topic. However, I can share with you some of my random thoughts about how your psychological makeup and your philosophical point of view can affect your trading, both in good and bad ways. While my comments are directed specifically at seasonals and seasonal trading, they apply equally to all trading systems and methods. Here are some points to consider when trading seasonals.

- *Is it necessary to "believe" in seasonals in order to use them effectively?* NO. Belief in a system or method is not the key consideration; however, it is helpful to see the validity of a concept and to have confidence in it. It is not necessary to believe in the concept as one might believe in religion. If you have examined the statistical efficacy and history of a system, method, or concept, and you believe the history to be accurate and valid as a means of trading, then all you need do is act in accordance with the historical results. Confidence is important, but it can only be attained through research.

- *The inability to "let go" is a very prevalent problem.* Many traders are afraid to let go. By this I mean that once a seasonal trade has been made, they're afraid to let the trade "do its thing." Win, lose, or draw, the die has been cast once a trade is established. But there are many traders who are insecure about the possible outcome of a trade. When the trade is going against them, they're fearful of a loss. And when the trade is going in their favor, they're afraid the profits will not continue. When it comes time to take a loss, they refuse to admit to the loss. Finally, when it comes time to take a profit they refuse to let go of the trade, hoping it will generate a larger profit if they hang on. All these problems and their associated difficulties are psychological issues caused by a lack of confidence, lack of experience, or lack of self-discipline. Any or all of the above can cause a good system to go bad.

- *Information overload is yet another problem.* There are those traders who feel that the more information they have, the better off they will be. I disagree. Sometimes less is more. Too much information can cause you to abandon your trading plan, particularly if you're a trader who lacks discipline. In such cases you must take the philosophical approach that your system or method is just as good as any system. And once you have taken this attitude, you will be more likely to ignore all but the most cogent and reliable inputs.

- *The view that history and life repeat can be very helpful in fostering confidence in seasonal trades and concepts.* Applying the logic of history to seasonals, you will quickly see that they are valid and worth pursuing. Interestingly enough, this historical perspective also holds true for other market patterns such as the Elliott Wave, Gann angles, etc.

- *The inability to complete a relationship* or interaction in interpersonal relationships is often reflected by a trader's inability to complete a relationship in the market. Such people have difficulty following through a trade from start to finish according to plan.

- *The importance of simplicity.* Many people feel that complicated systems are, by their very nature, better than simple systems. This view is common in the West, where we have been brainwashed into thinking that if something is computerized, complicated, and expensive, or based on highly scientific principles, that it must ipso facto be worthwhile. This is not necessarily the case. I believe that simple, basic and observable facts work best in the markets. In order to be a better trader, I suggest that you reject all that tends to obfuscate, and return to basics. Seasonality is a simple concept. It must be used in simple ways.

Day-of-Week Patterns in the Stock Market

 In his classic book *Don't Sell Stocks on Monday* (Facts on File), Yale Hirsch makes a powerful case supporting the statement made in the title of his book. Hirsch demonstrated statistically that stocks tend to make lows on Mondays. Arthur Merrill in his book *The Behavior of Prices on Wall Street* made a strong case for date-specific trades in the stock market. My chapter on seasonality gave you a number of high-odds seasonal trades specifically based

on exact entry and exit trades. Is it reasonable to extrapolate from the work of Hirsch and Merrill that there might be reliable and predictable patterns in the stock market based on day-of-week relationships?

The fact that many traders believe in the validity of such relationships is expressed in the statements they make. Such expressions as "turn-around Tuesday" are a reflection of traders' beliefs. But there are many market myths that are not reflected in reality once these beliefs are subjected to the cold and hard scrutiny of statistical analysis.

I subjected the day-of-week relationships to numerous statistical tests within the context of my Setup, Trigger, and Follow-Through method. What I learned was both surprising and ultimately very lucrative. The details of my discovery are presented in this chapter.

▶ The Basics

The basic method is simple indeed. The first step is to examine the relationship between the opening price and the closing price in S&P futures on Friday (or the last trading day of the week if the market is closed on Friday). As an alternative you can use either the Spyder (SPY), which is the stock equivalent of the S&P 500 or the Diamonds (DIA). Use only the day-session data for the purpose of determining this relationship.

To clarify, Figure 8.1 illustrates what I mean by the opening and the closing prices. As you can see, in this case the closing price is lower than the opening price. Note that there are only three possibilities for the relationship between the opening and the closing price of any given day. They are as follows:

Close is greater than the open	$C > O$
Close is less than the open	$C < O$
Close is equal to the open	$C = O$

FIGURE 8.1 ▶ Daily Price Bar

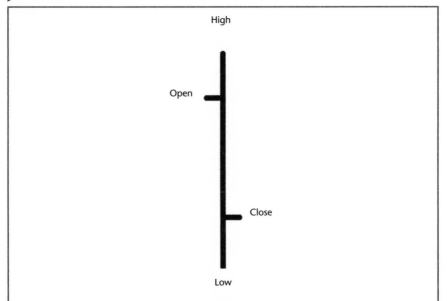

Daily price bar showing the open, high, low, and closing prices. In this case the closing price is LOWER than the opening price.

SETUP #1: IF CLOSE AND OPEN ARE THE SAME

First deal with the condition under which the closing and the opening price are EXACTLY the same. When I say EXACTLY, I mean EXACTLY that. This condition tells us that there will be NO trade. This condition, although it is relatively rare, tells us that there will be NO trade on Monday (or the first trading day of the week if the market is closed on Monday).

SETUP #2: IF CLOSE IS GREATER THAN THE OPEN

This condition signals a buy setup for Monday. Although there is a buy setup, note that the presence of a setup does NOT indicate that a trade has triggered. This is a very important point. Please do not forget it!

.05	+1.3	BL		IntTE	9.69	+.04	+2.1	IM		FF2010 n	13.12	−.07	+1.4	BL		FndotAmY	25.20	−.14	+5.0	MC		MigSeus
.03	+2.5	IL		Mgdln	9.35	+.02	+4.0	AB		FF2020 n	13.07	−.11	+1.0	XC		GlobalA	35.41	+.07	+6.3	GL		SmlCapGr
.09	+.9	BL		STGvSec	7.11		+1.1	SU		FF2030 n	12.99	−.14	+5	XC		OverseasA	19.59	+.04	+7.8	IL		SmallCo
.10	+.3	XC														SoGenGold n15.85		+.55	−9.0	AL		USGovSec

If the setup for a buy has developed, the next step is to place an order to BUY at a given amount ABOVE the HIGH of Friday. This order is placed as a buy stop order above the market. Figure 8.2 is an illustration of what the procedure looks like on a price chart.

SETUP #3: IF CLOSE IS LESS THAN OPEN

This condition sets up a possible sell signal for Monday. If the sell setup occurs, this does NOT mean that you will sell short on Monday. In order to sell short on Monday you will need a trigger. The trigger for the sell trade is for the market to trade below the Friday low. Unless the market trades below the Friday low by a

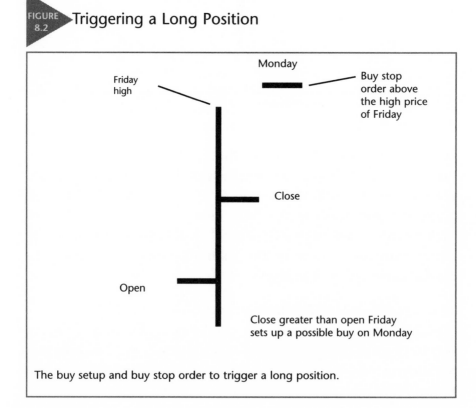

FIGURE 8.2 ▶ Triggering a Long Position

The buy setup and buy stop order to trigger a long position.

FIGURE
8.3
Setup and Trigger

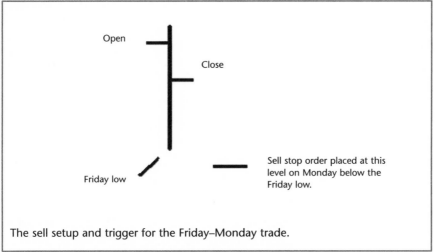

The sell setup and trigger for the Friday–Monday trade.

given amount, the trade is not triggered on the short side. This is a very important point. Please do not forget it. On a chart, this relationship appears as shown in Figure 8.3.

Follow-Through

Now that you know how this trade triggers, the next step is follow-through. Follow-through consists of two parts, the stop loss and the profit target. Let's first deal with the stop loss.

My many years in the markets have taught me that there are two kinds of stop losses a trader or investor can use. I call them the "dumb stop" and the "smart stop."

▶ The "Dumb Stop"

As you may well know, myths abound in the stock and futures markets. Traders and investors are often predisposed to magical and superstitious thinking. I won't waste your time by citing any of these, since to do so may pollute your mind. You are better off never hearing these myths, because you may begin to believe them! The "dumb stop" is a stop loss that is placed on the basis of how much money you can afford to lose if your stock pick is incorrect. Think about how absurd this procedure is! Buying a stock and placing a risk level on that stock is not like buying a piece of furniture within the constraints of your budget. The stock market doesn't care at all about what you can afford to risk on a stock. There are thousands of traders who want to risk only a few hundred dollars on a stock. They place a stop loss very close to their buy or sell price and they're surprised when they get stopped out over and over again! The size of your stop loss must be based on the behavior of the stock or the stock market. It must be based on the system or method or market indicators you are using and NOT on what you can afford to risk. As I said earlier, the market has no concern for what you can or cannot afford to lose on a stock. In fact, we find that in many cases larger stop losses produce larger profits and more accurate trades.

Perhaps an example will help illustrate my point. Note also that this very important fact applies to virtually all aspects of investing above and beyond the method I'm describing. In other words, you can adapt the concept I am about to share with you to just about any investment or trading method you are using.

Shown in tabular form in Figure 8.4 are the results of a given trading methodology using different stop-loss levels. Note the progression of profits in relation to size of stop as well as percentage accuracy in relation to stop-loss size. The larger the stop grows, the more accurate the system and the larger the profits. Think about this the next time you tell yourself "I think I'll buy this stock and use a very small stop." This kind of thinking is an invitation to losing money.

Figure 8.4 clearly illustrates the point I've been making about stop losses. As you can see, the accuracy as well as the total profits and the average profit per trade grow as the stop-loss size increases.

FIGURE 8.4 Performance of a Trading System at Different Stop-Loss Levels

QQQ Short-Term Trading System

Results at Different Stop-Loss Levels

Stop Loss $	Net Profit	% Correct	Avg Trade
$500	$1,410	58.20%	$11
$750	$3,415	68.40%	$26
$1,000	$9,080	74.20%	$69
$1,500	$18,005	81.90%	$142
$2,000	$21,375	83.60%	$174
$2,500	$23,205	85.00%	$193
$3,000	$25,420	85.80%	$212
No Stop	$25,420	85.80%	$212

Eventually the stop size reaches the point at which raising the stop loss no longer has a positive impact on results. This analysis is not an anomaly. It holds true for virtually every trading system or method. You would do well to heed its lesson and meaning. Accordingly, the stop loss you use on the Friday-Monday trading method should not be the "dumb stop" based on what you can afford, but rather the "smart stop," which is based on market behavior and the system itself.

▶ The Smart Stop

The smart stop for this trading method is a dollar-risk stop or a percentage stop of the entry price. To determine the correct stop loss for a given stock, you will need to do some historical testing, or you can use the suggestions in this chapter.

Follow-Through: Profitable Exit

Now that you know the setup, the trigger, and the stop-loss method for this pattern, let's take a look at the profitable exit strategy. In

.05	+1.3	BL	IntlTE	9.69	+.04	+2.1	IM	FF2010n	13.12	−.07	+1.4	BL	FndofAmY	25.20	−.14	+5.0	MC	MigSecs	
.03	+2.5	IL	Mgdln	9.35	+.02	+4.0	AB	FF2020n	13.07	−.11	+1.0	XC	GlobalA	35.41	+.07	+6.3	GL	SmlCapGr	
.09	+.9	BL	STGvSec	7.11		+1.1	SU	FF2030n	12.99	−.14	+.5	XC	OverseasA	19.59	+.04	+7.8	IL	SmallCo	
.10	+.3	XC											SoGenGold	15.85	+.55	−.9.0	ALI	USGovSec	

addition to the setup, trigger, and stop loss follow-through, the key aspect to the Friday-Monday strategy is the exit. The exit is unique—very few trading systems or methods employ a strategy such as this one. The exit strategy is to close out the Friday-Monday trade on the first profitable opening (FPO). This most interesting strategy is highly effective in that, by its very nature, it increases the percentage accuracy of the trading strategy. By virtually forcing exit at a profit (unless a trade is stopped out first), this approach increases accuracy drastically. The other side of the FPO coin is that it can also limit profits considerably. To counteract this tendency, the FPO is best used in markets or stocks where volatility is high. This is why I suggest using the Friday-Monday strategy with FPO in stocks such as the SPY, QQQ, and/or DIA, or in higher-priced stocks that tend to make large moves over relatively short periods of time.

FPO means exactly what its name implies. If your trade OPENS at a profit by ANY AMOUNT, then you exit at the market. You do NOT wait, you do not place a trailing stop, you do not attempt to project a profit target, and you just get out at the market. To clarify, FPO means that you will exit on any opening price that is above the price at which you bought the stock if you entered a long position. It's that simple and it's that complicated. Why do I say it's complicated? I say this because, in my experience, traders will almost always want to find a way to change the procedure in efforts to improve it. If you want to do this, then do lots of research and don't trade this method until you've completed your work.

The exit strategy for a short position is the same, only in reverse. Because you will have been short, you will buy back your short position on the first profitable opening. Many times the exit of either a short or a long position will be on the next day; however, the trade could last for a few days.

Let's take a look at the overall strategy for the buy and sell signals using the Friday-Monday method. Figures 8.5 and 8.6 provide a visual representation of each signal. Remember that we do not

FIGURE 8.5

The Friday-Monday Sell STF

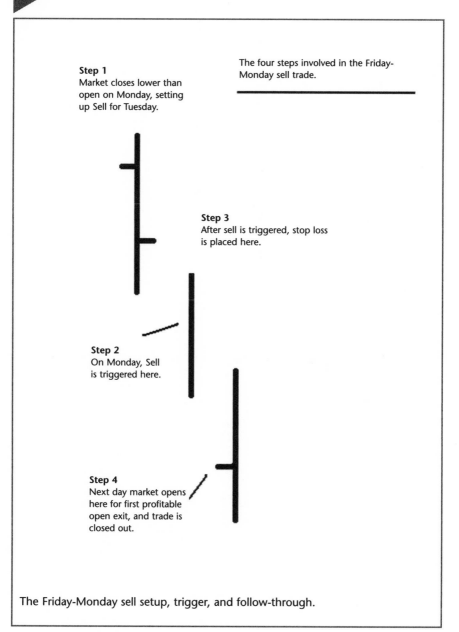

The four steps involved in the Friday-Monday sell trade.

Step 1
Market closes lower than open on Monday, setting up Sell for Tuesday.

Step 3
After sell is triggered, stop loss is placed here.

Step 2
On Monday, Sell is triggered here.

Step 4
Next day market opens here for first profitable open exit, and trade is closed out.

The Friday-Monday sell setup, trigger, and follow-through.

FIGURE 8.6 ► The Friday-Monday Buy Pattern

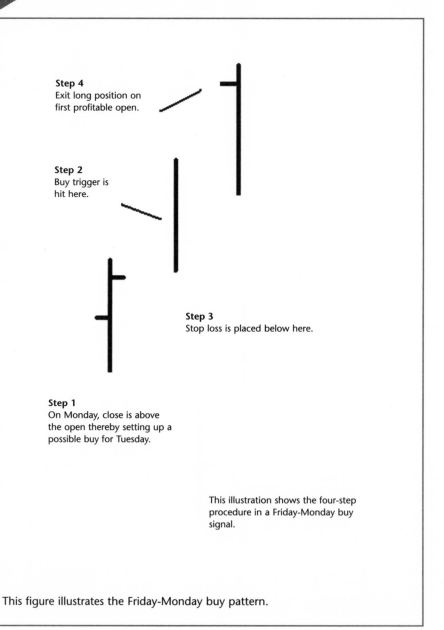

Step 4
Exit long position on
first profitable open.

Step 2
Buy trigger is
hit here.

Step 3
Stop loss is placed below here.

Step 1
On Monday, close is above
the open thereby setting up a
possible buy for Tuesday.

This illustration shows the four-step
procedure in a Friday-Monday buy
signal.

This figure illustrates the Friday-Monday buy pattern.

use the 24-hour or after-market-trading for this method. We use the day session only!

▶ Sample Trades

Figures 8.7 and 8.8 show buys and/or trades in several stocks. I have marked the entry and exit signals in each case. Please take a few minutes to review these charts to make certain that you are clear on the methodology. Note also that the triggers and stops for each of these stocks are different, because these values are a function of the underlying behavior of these stocks.

FIGURE 8.7 ▶ The Friday-Monday Pattern in Siebel Systems

 FIGURE 8.8 The Friday-Monday Pattern in DIA

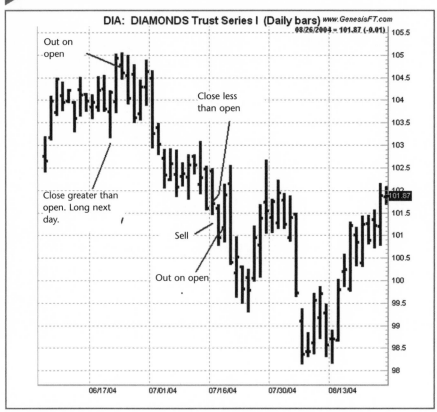

Performance

The performance of this method varies as a function of the input variables you select. In most cases the accuracy of this approach has been in the 75 percent area, although it can be considerably higher if you use a larger step loss.

CHAPTER

9

Surfing the Stock Channel

Markets often move in trends. While some traders and market analysts would argue that markets spend most of their time moving about in random directions, others would vehemently disagree. Those who claim that price behavior is random are proponents of the so-called "random walk theory." This view of the market holds that you can make money in the market by simply picking stocks at random and managing your risk. It suggests that there is no advantage to picking stocks. Indeed, evidence could be marshaled to support both arguments, but I believe that the random walk theory is incorrect. It is not my purpose in this book to debate the merits or flaws in each of these diametrically opposed points of view. Without a doubt, my vote is in favor of stock-picking and the use of market trends as methods of profitable trading and/or investing.

The method described in this chapter makes use of market trends. It attempts to take advantage of market trends in order to generate profits. Before I can tell you the details of this method, I need to teach you about trends and how to find them.

▶ What Is a Trend?

Trend is another word for direction. A trend or market direction can be either up, down, or sideways. What may constitute an uptrend in one time frame may in fact be a small portion of a bigger downtrend. By this I mean that trends are relevant to the time frame in which they occur. Consider the fact that the stock market may be in the throes of a large decline that has been in existence for three years. Within the context of this lengthy decline in stocks, the market might stage a very large recovery that lasts for two days. Without knowing the larger trend of the market, someone who only had an opportunity to see the two-day recovery might incorrectly assume that the larger trend was up. The trend of a stock or of the market in general is a function of time frames.

If you are a long-term investor, your time frame might be two years or even ten years. You may not be at all concerned with what happens today or even over the next few months, because you are focused on the long term. You're more interested in where your investments will be ten years down the road than one year, six months, or six days from now. You're willing to ride the long-term trend. In order to do so effectively, you must also

5 +1.3	BL	IntTE	9.69	+.04 +2.1	IM	FF2010n	13.12	−.07 +1.4	BL	FndofAmY	25.20	−.14 +5.0	MC	MidCapIdx	
3 +2.5	IL	Mgdln	9.35	+.02 +4.0	AB	FF2020n	13.07	−.11 +1.0	XC	GlobalA	35.41	+.07 +6.3	GL	SmlCapGro	1
9 +.9	BL	STGvSec	7.11	+1.1	SU	FF2030n	12.99	−.14 +.5	XC	OverseasA	19.59	+.04 +7.8	IL	SmallCo	1
0 +.3	XC									SoGenGoldn	15.85	+.55 −9.0	ALI	USGovSecs	1

be willing to overlook the short-term and intermediate-term trends. You will need to ignore short-term bad news because your time horizon stretcher is much longer than the next few days or months.

As a short-term trader, however, you are concerned with the trend of prices over the next few days or weeks, while you may not be at all concerned about the longer-term trend. Is it possible to wear both hats at the same time? Yes, indeed it is, but you will need to be disciplined and clear in your objectives. There is no rule or law or requirement that you can only do one type of investing and not another.

On the far end of the trading continuum we have the day trader. Day traders are only interested in what happens during the course of the day. Their time perspective is the shortest term of all market participants. To the day trader, a trade that lasts for several days is an eternity, because it is their goal to be in and out of trades by the end of the day. What's right for the day trader is not necessarily right for the investor or intermediate-term trader. It may not even be right for the short-term trader.

Figures 9.1, 9.2, and 9.3 show market trends in three different time frames for several stocks.

As you can see, there are different perspectives on market trends. Each approach has its positive and negative aspects. Yet all traders and investors are ultimately concerned about trends, because the trend is what will bring you either profits or losses. In order to make money you must know how to find the trend accurately. In addition, you must know how to determine when a trend is likely to change and/or when it has changed.

Market analysts and traders have developed a plethora of tools to achieve these goals. I will discuss some of them shortly. For now, however, let's look at topics that are just as important as the trend. These two topics are support and resistance. Support and resistance are part and parcel of a trend.

FIGURE
9.1

Downtrends within Existing Uptrend

FIGURE 9.2 ▶ Uptrend within Existing Downtrend

GGNS: Genus, Inc. (Daily bars)

www.GenesisFT.com
08/20/2004 = 2.00 (-0.02)

The daily trend in this stock is down, but during the downtrend a small uptrend develops.

The very short-term trend is up within a larger downtrend.

Jul-04   Aug-04   Sep-04

FIGURE 9.3 ▶ IBM Ten-Minute Chart

The ten-minute chart for IBM shows the major uptrend with smaller up- and down-trends as part of the larger trend.

▶ Defining Support and Resistance

The terms support and resistance mean what they normally do. Support is a price or price range within which a given market is likely to stop its decline. From this level the market is expected to move higher. As it moves higher, it may establish new support levels which, at least in theory, should keep the price of the stock from declining. Hence, if investors or traders knew that the trend of a market was up, and if they knew where the support level was for that market, then they could buy in the support area and, at least in theory, make a profit.

Resistance is the opposite of support. When the trend of a stock or given market is declining, the stock tends to return to resistance levels where traders can sell it short (see Figure 9.4).

FIGURE 9.4 ▶ Three Distinct Weekly Trends in Sunoco

Examples of Support and Resistance

There are many ways in which traders attempt to determine support and resistance. Some of these are very effective, while others are marginal at best. The most typical way of determining support and resistance is through the use of trendlines. Trendlines are very simple to determine, but they are not very effective at determining support and resistance levels. Figure 9.5 illustrates the use of trendlines.

 FIGURE 9.5 Drawing Support and Resistance Lines

To draw a support trendline, simply draw a straight line under price lows on a bar chart. To draw a resistance trendline, draw a straight line above price highs on a bar chart.

FIGURE 9.6 ▸ Support and Resistance Lines

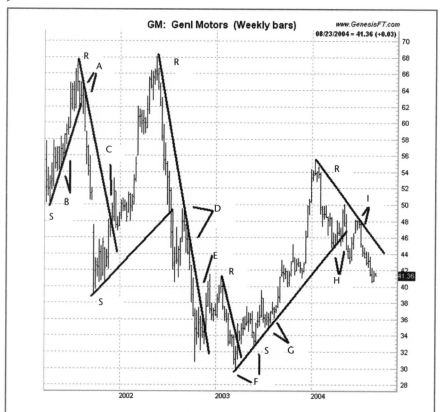

GM: Genl Motors (Weekly bars)

www.GenesisFT.com
08/23/2004 = 41.36 (+0.03)

This illustration shows the following: S stands for support trendlines and R for resistance trendlines.

In Figure 9.6, at point B the stock hits trendline support a number of times and then rallies. The trend continues higher until point A, when a down trendline is established and resistance is hit a number of times. The stock then falls below the support trendline and declines rapidly until a new support line is formed. Points D and E indicate tests of resistance where the stock could have been sold. Declines to a support trendline occur at points F and G. At point H support is tested again. Prices decline below

.05 +1.3	BL	IntTE	9.69	+.04 +2.1	IM	FF2010n	13.12	-.07 +1.4	BL	FndofAmY	25.20	-.14 +5.0	MC	MidSec
.03 +2.5	IL	Mgdln	9.35	+.02 +4.0	AB	FF2020n	13.07	-.11 +1.0	XC	GlobalA	35.41	+.07 +6.3	GL	SmiCapGr
.09 +.9	BL	STGvSec	7.11	+1.1	SU	FF2030n	12.99	-.14 +.5	XC	OverseasA	19.59	+.04 +7.8	IL	SmallCo
.10 +.3	XC									SoGenGold n15.85	+.55 -9.0	AU	USGovSec

support and a new down trendline develops with resistance hit at point I.

The trader who followed trendline support, resistance, and trend could have bought or sold at the indicated support and resistance points. The good news about using this method is that AFTER THE FACT, it looks good. However, when you are actually attempting to trade using the method day by day (or within any time frame), there are often issues as to where the trendline should be drawn, how much deviation from the line is acceptable, and more important, what is the trend?

Moving Average Support and Resistance

Because markets are dynamic, and traditional trendline analysis, as described earlier, does not perform as well as we would like, the use of moving average support, resistance, and trend is more popular among traders. A moving average (MA) is determined by adding up the last X number of prices and dividing by the total number of prices used. Hence, a ten-day moving average is determined by adding the last ten closing prices of a stock and dividing by ten. The average "moves" because the next day you drop the oldest day in the data and add the current day. The moving average is, therefore, a dynamic tool that adjusts to the market trend. The trendline is static because it does not similarly adjust to changing price conditions.

As an example of how moving average trends are more reliable in stocks than trendlines, consider the same chart as shown in Figure 9.7, but this time with a moving average used as support and resistance instead of a trendline. See Figure 9.8 for this comparison.

In the stock market, traders and investors have used different lengths of moving averages depending on the length of time they want to be in the given stocks. Traders can change the length of the moving average (MA) to suit their particular needs. One of the more popular moving averages used in the stock market is the 200-day moving average. Supposedly, this moving average is the

The 200-Day MA Results for SPY

FIGURE 9.7

Overall

Total Net Profit:	$118,720	Profit Factor ($Wins/$Losses):	**3.60**
Total Trades:	41	Winning Percentage:	**26.8%**
Average Trade:	$2,896	Payout Ratio (Avg Win/Loss):	**9.82**
Avg # of Bars in Trade:	96.17	Z-Score (W/L Predictability):	0.2
Avg # of Trades per Year:	2.6	Percent in the Market:	94.6%
Max Closed-out Drawdown:	-$18,470	Max Intraday Drawdown:	-$23,660
Account Size Required:	$23,660	Return Pct:	**501.8%**
Open Equity:	-$580	Kelly Ratio:	0.1938
Current Streak:	2 Wins	Optimal f:	0.49

Winning Trades		**Losing Trades**	
Total Winners:	11	Total Losers:	30
Gross Profit:	$164,340	Gross Loss:	-$45,620
Average Win:	$14,940	Average Loss:	-$1,521
Largest Win:	$37,750	Largest Loss:	-$6,440
Largest Drawdown in Win:	-$5,190	Largest Peak in Loss:	$12,400
Avg Drawdown in Win:	-$1,200	Avg Peak in Loss:	$1,824
Avg Run Up in Win:	$23,917	Avg Run Up in Loss:	$1,824
Avg Run Down in Win:	-$1,200	Avg Run Down in Loss:	-$1,791
Most Consec Wins:	2	Most Consec Losses:	11
Avg # of Consec Wins:	1.22	Avg # of Consec Losses:	3.75
Avg # of Bars in Wins:	299.55	Avg # of Bars in Losses:	21.60

Note that this strategy assumes that 1,000 shares were traded each time.

one that is best used for determining the trend of the overall stock market, as well as the direction of the market trend.

▶ Debunking the Myths

In the stock market, as in many other fields of endeavor, myths abound. For example, thousands (perhaps millions) of investors believe that the 200-day MA is important in determining the trend of the stock market as well as the support and resistance levels of the stock market. Some traders believe this is also true for individual stocks. If we separate reality from myth, we often find that what

FIGURE
9.8

Weekly General Motors Chart

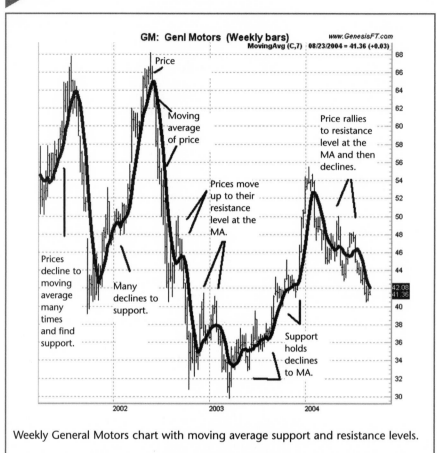

Weekly General Motors chart with moving average support and resistance levels.

most people believe about the market is just not true at all. The 200-day MA is another example of how myths pervade investor and trader thinking. The way we think is often reflected in how we trade.

The much revered 200-day MA, when subjected to a solid and thorough test of accuracy fails to meet expectations. In fact, my test indicated less than 15 percent accuracy using the 200-day MA as a timing method with the DIA (stock equivalent of the Dow Jones Industrial Average).

▶ A Better Method

A much better method is to use the High Low Moving Average Channel (MAC). This method does not use the closing price of a stock , rather it uses two moving averages, one of the high price and one of the low price. When used in this fashion the two moving averages for a high-low channel that I call the MAC. The MAC provides us with the following information about a stock:

- Support and resistance
- Trend
- Trend strength or weakness
- Buy signal
- Sell signal, and
- Volatility

By plotting the channel on a chart (see Figure 9.9), we can determine all of the above factors. I have illustrated and identified all of these accordingly.

Here are the rules for implementing the MAC.

- Use a 10.MA of highs and an 8.MA of lows
- Two consecutive price bars entirely above the high of the MAC suggests a change in trend from down to up
- In an up trend as defined above, the low of the MAC tends to serve as support and is often a good buying point
- A narrowing MAC in an up trend tends to suggest a correction to support or a top
- A widening MAC in an up trend tends to precede a surge to higher prices
- Two consecutive price bars entirely below the low of the MAC suggests a change in trend from up to down
- In a down trend as defined above, the high of the MAC tends to serve as resistance and is often a selling buying point
- A narrowing MAC in a down trend tends to suggest a correction to resistance or a bottom

FIGURE 9.9 — High Low Moving Average Channel (MAC)

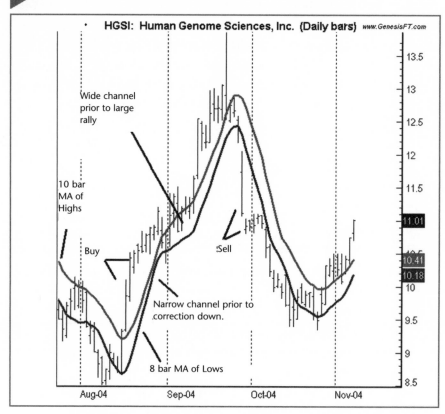

HGSI: Human Genome Sciences, Inc. (Daily bars) www.GenesisFT.com

Wide channel prior to large rally

10 bar MA of Highs

Buy

Sell

Narrow channel prior to correction down.

8 bar MA of Lows

13.5
13
12.5
12
11.5
11.01
10.41
10.18
10
9.5
9
8.5

Aug-04   Sep-04   Oct-04   Nov-04

- A widening MAC in a down trend tends to precede a drop to lower prices
- The more consecutive bars entirely above the channel, the more bullish is the trend
- The more consecutive bars entirely below the bottom of the channel, the more bearish is the trend

It is best to use the MAC with another non-correlated timing or trend indicator such as momentum or stochastics. If you work with the MAC you will discover even more applications. Note that the MAC can be used in all time frames.

CHAPTER

10

Discipline and Trader Psychology

None of the excellent methods discussed in this book will work for you unless you have solid discipline. Application of these methods is just as important as the methods themselves. Unless you have mastered the third step in the STF structure, you will never succeed as an investor or as a trader. To assist you in this effort, I will share some of the observations I have made about my trading as well as what I have learned about how most individuals trade. Do not discount what I am about to tell you by assuming that none of this applies to you.

▶ Enemies of the Trader

Trading stock for the short term is, at best, a difficult undertaking and at worst, a losing proposition. Even so the allure, intrigue, and the possibility of striking it rich continue to attract traders the world over. As Jesse Livermore (alias Edwin LeFevbre) so eloquently stated in his book, "The chief enemies of the trader are always boring from within." What or who are these "chief enemies"? How can we recognize them? There are many roadblocks to successful stock trading. In fact, several books could be written about the factors that limit success. In general terms, however, I've summarized the major factors for you as follows. While I'm sure there will be many who disagree with my conclusions, here is a synopsis of my opinions, followed by a brief commentary about each.

Imagination

Traders are prone to overly active imaginations. They imagine positive as well as negative scenarios. Both can be destructive because they may lead to unrealistic conclusions and expectations. It is best for the trader to avoid imagining possible outcomes for a given trade. Imagination is a wonderful gift for writing books, making movies and other forms of art, but it has no place in trading other than, perhaps, in the area of system development. Once you have entered a trade, do not allow your imagination to rule your emotions.

Over-Thinking

Over-thinking is an aspect of the overly active imagination but in more concrete terms. Once you have developed a trading system and have entered a trade, all the thinking in the world won't change the outcome of that trade. Avoid creating "if-then" scenarios. Avoid talking or thinking in phrases such as "If I had only," or "I should have," or "What if," or "If I added more indicators to my system, then. . . ." This type of analysis should be done when developing a system, NOT after a trade has been entered and NOT after your system has indicated that a trade should be entered.

News

Traders have a love-hate relationship with news. They love the news when it supports their position in the market(s), and they hate the news when it is contrary to their position in the market(s). Unless you know the news before it happens and unless you're the person making the news, the odds are that it won't help you. There are too many insiders who know the news before you do. As market technicians, we expect that our indicators will alert us to when markets will turn. In this way, technical indicators tell us the impact of the news and not the news itself. Try to avoid listening to the news if you are prone to be swayed to deviate from your system or trading plan. The news can be your best friend and your worst enemy. Try to avoid either of these extremes.

Fear

The time to be fearful about a trade is BEFORE you enter it. Once it has been entered, your fate is sealed. Let the trade go to its logical conclusion as dictated by your system or method. Don't get out too soon and don't get out too late. Simply stated, follow the rules and they will eliminate the fear.

Greed

Greed can also prove to be your greatest enemy. When it's time to get out of a trade, get out. Don't hold on, attempting to squeeze every last drop of money out of the trade. And please, please,

please don't accumulate a larger position on any market if your finances and risk won't allow it. Having too large a position at the wrong time can and will destroy you.

Expectation

The only expectation you should have as a trader is that you will lose money. Beyond this, any profit you make is a gift. Expect the worst-case scenario, not the best! Expectation falls into the category of "imagination," as discussed above.

Rationalization

Don't try to explain away your losses by resorting to all manner of excuses. You lost on a trade because your system or method was wrong or because you didn't follow the rules. You must assume full responsibility. There is always the temptation to blame your broker, or your trading advisor, or a newsletter writer, or a friend. Take full responsibility for your profits as well as your losses. There are no excuses. Most traders have a repertoire of excuses that amounts to a tired litany. Forget them—they don't work!

Disorganization

Try to be organized and disciplined in your work. If you use a system or method, make certain you update it on a timely basis. Keep good track of the trades you've made. Forgetting to enter or exit a trade due to disorganization can prove costly. Believe me—I know what I'm talking about!

I'm certain that there are other enemies as well. But here are what I consider to be the major impediments to the success of a trader. Study my list in light of your own personal experiences.

To Think or Not to Think: The Trader's Dilemma

In 1968, when I made my first stock market trade, thinking was fashionable. The 1960s and 1970s were good times for thinkers, free thinkers, thought-provoking issues, civil disobedience, and analytical traders. Thinkers thought great thoughts about the future of our nation, about our presence and purpose (if any) in Viet Nam, about domestic and international racial issues, about freedom and equality, about the poor and the homeless. Thinking prompted radical action by various political-interest groups. There were numerous and violent antiwar protests, a variety of civil disobedience events, draft card burnings, sit-ins and student protests. The stock and futures markets were studied closely. They were analyzed, scrutinized, and glamorized. Computer analysis of the markets was a new and promising science.

The "Zeitgeist"

Against the backdrop of this intellectual zeitgeist, we were taught that if success was to be attained as traders, we would need to consider each trade carefully; all potential outcomes were to be critically evaluated in terms of risk and reward. We were told that trading decisions, which were the result of intensive analysis were likely to be more correct than those which were the product of less-intensive scrutiny. In fact, thinking about trades was so much in vogue that traders would frequently seek out numerous sources of information in order to validate each of their trades. There was no such thing as "too much information." After all, how could there be too much information in the so-called Information Age?

▶ Edsel Trading

Do you remember the story of the Edsel? In what seemed to be a reasonable approach, the Ford Motor Company designed the Edsel to please the consumer. They did so by attempting to include everything that a buyer would want in a car. The end result was a car that failed miserably. The simple truth is that "too many cooks spoil the pie." Consider the following questions:

05 +1.3	BL	IntTE	9.69	+.04 +2.1	IM	FF2010n	13.12	-.07 +1.4	BL	FndofAmY	25.20	-.14 +5.0	MC	MgSecs	
03 +2.5	IL	Mgdin	9.35	+.02 +4.0	AB	FF2020n	13.07	-.11 +1.0	XC	GlobalA	35.41	+.07 +6.3	GL	SmlCapGr	
09 +.9	BL	STGvSec	7.11	+1.1	SU	FF2030n	12.99	-.14 +.5	XC	OverseasA	19.59	+.04 +7.8	IL	SmallCo	
10 +.3	XC									SoGenGold n15.85		+.55 -9.0	AL	USGovSec	

- How much information is enough?
- How can you decide when you have given a decision enough thought?
- Are there any objective measures by which you can know when you have thought about something enough, or does the process end when things "feel right"?
- Is there a correlation between the amount of thought devoted to a trade and its end result?
- Can intensive analysis and thought really lead to success in trading?

These questions are totally absurd. What is deep thought to one trader can be a passing notion to another trader, and a totally worthless activity to another. There are no set standards, no guarantees, and no insurance policies. There is no firm correlation between the amount of thought and deliberation that goes into a trade and the outcome of that trade. In fact, if there IS a correlation it's likely to be an inverse one.

Decisions made seemingly off the cuff by some traders are often more successful than decisions made by committees. And, of course, computers have totally revolutionized the decision-making process by doing our "thinking" for us. *Once the computer has done the hard work, there's really nothing left to do but take the prescribed action.* Any hesitation subsequent to the acquisition of knowledge is bound to lead to confusion, indecision, insecurity, ambivalence, and equivocation—none of which are constructive inputs to the formula for success.

Why Bother?

The purpose of my comments is to make a case for simpler and "less intelligent" trading. Once the facts are known and the computer has decided the best course of action, there's no choice but to act. Failure to do so constitutes a breach of contract between you and the computer, but more important, between you and yourself.

5 +1.3	BL	InITE	9.69	+.04 +2.1	IM	FF2010n	13.12	-.07 +1.4	BL	FndofAmY	25.20	-.14 +5.0	MC	MgSecs
3 +2.5	IL	Mgdln	9.35	+.02 +4.0	AB	FF2020n	13.07	-.11 +1.0	XC	GlobalA	35.41	+.07 +6.3	GL	SmlCapGro 1
9 +.9	BL	STGvSec	7.11	+1.1	SU	FF2030n	12.99	-.14 +.5	XC	OverseasA	19.59	+.04 +7.8	IL	SmallCo 1

I suggest that a failure to act on your system is the first indication that you have taken a wrong turn, which will eventually lead you down the road to ruin.

The only way that learning can develop is through action. Non-behavior, on the other hand, means that there will be no learning, regardless of whether the action would have produced positive or negative results.

Have you ever noticed the relationship between the success of a trader and his or her ability to take action, right or wrong? Traders who make decisions promptly and without fear most often come out ahead in the long run. Furthermore, it's been my observation that there's an inverse correlation between intellectual ability and market success—the smarter you are (or think you are), the more you'll think, and the less money you'll make.

I'm not saying that you have to be stupid in order to trade well. What I am saying is that you can't overanalyze a trade or you may be too late to make it, or you'll talk yourself out of it. Traders who can act quickly, evaluating information and reacting to it on a gut level, are often traders who succeed. While I am not advocating irrational or impulsive behavior with your money, I am saying that ONCE THE FACTS ARE IN, THEY'RE IN. The methods taught in this book are totally objective. They do not require you to think too long, but they do demand prompt and decisive action.

It is the fear of being wrong that inhibits action. But if this fear also keeps you from making decisions, then you had better give up the game—there's no way you can play it without taking some heat. You never know ahead of time whether your decision will be profitable or not. If you did, there would be no game. There would be no losers to help sustain the winners.

▶ Feelings Aren't Facts!

Have you observed a relationship between your feelings about a given trade and its eventual success or failure? Consider this: The more a trade scares you, the more likely it is to be successful. The trades you're scared out of are often the ones that work. WHY? The human brain cannot think without being bombarded by external interference and influences.

Any intellectual process involved in making a trading decision is subject to a thousand and one fears before the thought becomes translated into action. To give in to those fears is to circumvent the system.

Trade—Don't Think

Consider the following list of blunders that are ordinarily considered the by-products of informed thought. Then think about how much money you've lost or failed to make as a result of these "crimes of thinking."

- *There's too much risk.* This is basically a rationalization for fear. It's been said that "you don't know how deep a hole is until you stand in it." This applies to the risk of trading as well. If it's the degree of dollar risk that's bothering you, there are many ways this problem may be resolved. Risk can be decreased by the use of options and/or options strategies. Risk evaluation is an intangible. If intangibles scare you, don't drive a car. If you really think—and think some more—about what could happen to you on an expressway, you'll not want to drive. If you think about the risk of trading, you won't want to trade.

- *I don't feel good about this trade. It scares me.* Here's a favorite cop-out on the list of excuses. Assuming that your signal to trade came from a computer or mechanical trading system, then this excuse is without merit. Your computer had no idea that you wouldn't like the trade. Nor does the computer care about your feelings. Following feelings or "The Force" may have been good for Luke Sykwalker, but it's a totally bogus approach when signals come from a mechanical system or a computer.

- *The trade looks good but. . .* Here's a worthless bit of reasoning. The signal looks good but. . . BUT WHAT? You want to get in cheaper. . . you want to wait for a pullback . . . you want more confirmation. . . you want to wait for a report. . . you want to wait for the next signal. . . . you want to talk to your broker first. . . EXCUSES! All poor excuses, the bastard children of what you think is sharp thinking! You might as well wait to ask your dead grandfather if the trade's good.

- *Let's see how the market opens before I enter my order.* Let's check it after the first hour of trading. . . let's put in an order below the market. . . above the market. This is an excuse I've used hundreds of times. IT'S ALL NONSENSE! These are the fatherless children of the blunder that comes of too much thinking. Short-term stock trading is very much a game of stimulus and response. The signal is your stimulus, and you must make the proper response.

- *"It just doesn't look right."* Here's the real *thinking* trader's excuse. And it's another totally worthless one. This one comes from truly deep thought. It comes from an analysis of the economy, trends, possibly even volume and open interest, and of course, from the input of too many traders and advisors. It you want to get totally confused and frozen into inaction, think about all the facts and opinions, evaluate them, throw them into the hopper, and decide that you can't decide because something just doesn't seem right.

▶ I'm Far from Perfect

Don't think for even one second that I'm preaching to you from a position of perfection. I've made more than my share of mistakes. And I'll continue to make mistakes as long as I live. My hope, however, is that I'll make fewer and less serious ones. And that's my hope for you as well.

Try a little experiment. Make a commitment to take the next ten trades without thinking about them. Just follow your system(s) to the letter without giving them any thought. After you've done this, evaluate your results. See how you've done. See how you feel. Here's what I expect you'll find: You'll have spent less valuable time on meaningless thought; you'll have made the trades you were supposed to make; you'll feel better about yourself, more confident and more secure; and you'll probably have made money as well.

20/20 Hindsight

We all tend to look back upon situations as "Monday morning quarterbacks." In the cold light of objectivity, everything we should have done or could have done often becomes clear. As long as this process results in learning, I encourage you to engage in it. However, if the process becomes an excuse for breast-beating or for rationalizing errors, you're simply wasting your time.

We are all guilty of using 20/20 hindsight. We are all guilty of the "I Should Have" syndrome. Consider the following statements, all of which should be familiar to you, either as they appear here, or in countless variations on their themes:

- I knew the market was bottoming; *I should* have gone long when I wanted to.
- *I should* have used a stop loss. My system was right.
- *I should* have added to my position. I knew it was the right thing to do.
- *I should* have done what the charts were telling me to do. Getting out of my position because of the bearish news was clearly not the right thing.
- *I should* have put on my position and closed my eyes to the day-to-day news developments.
- *I should* have sold short and gone fishing.
- *I should* have done my homework. Two days after I stopped following my technical indicators, the market started one of its largest moves in history.

- *I should* have traded with blinders on. . . my own feelings and analyses are best.

This is just a partial list of the "should haves" that are part and parcel of the 20/20 hindsight that all traders have. There are thousands of traders who KNEW when stocks would top, who knew when interest rates would top, who KNEW when gold would bottom, but who didn't do a thing about it.

In fact, these same individuals may, to make matters worse, have lost money in spite of the fact that they KNEW what the right action was, and KNEW what was going to happen.

Why didn't they do what they should have done? This is, to be sure, the key issue. This is the issue that has haunted traders and investors for hundreds, if not thousands of years. And it will continue to plague all of us for hundreds of years to come.

What's the answer? What follows will, I hope, help shed some light on at least one aspect of the problem.

▶ Information Overload

Way back in the early 1980s, as the gold market was making its long-term top, the market was, as you can well imagine, extremely volatile. Emotions ran high. Incredibly bullish forecasts were an almost daily event. Talk of $1000, even $2000 gold was common.

Expectations of $100 silver (then about $45/oz.) were also common, perpetuated in part by the very bullish public prognostications of Bunker Hunt. One of the most well-attended investment seminars was held in Dallas, near the peak of the gold and silver markets.

The RealMoney One conference featured dozens of traders, advisors, and other market experts commenting on the precious metals. As you can surmise, most analysts were bullish. As bullish as they were, they differed as to how high they expected gold and silver would go.

Once the seminar was over and I had delivered my opinion to the crowd, I entered the elevator. As I waited for the elevator doors

.05	+1.3	BL		IntTE	9.68	+.04	+2.1	IM		FF2010n	13.12	−.07	+1.4	BL		FndotAmY	25.20	−.14	+5.0	MC		MgSecs
.03	+2.5	IL		Mgdln	9.35	+.02	+4.0	AB		FF2020n	13.07	−.11	+1.0	XC		GlobalA	35.41	+.07	+6.3	GL		SmiCapGr
.09	+.9	BL		STGvSec	7.11		+1.1	SU		FF2030n	12.99	−.14	+.5	XC		OverseasA	19.59	+.04	+7.8	IL		SmallCo
.10	+.3	XC														SoGenGdn	15.85	+.55	−.90	AU		USGovSec

to close, another man entered. He looked dazed and confused. We spoke briefly.

I commented that he looked upset. He told me that he had come to the conference expecting answers. Instead, he got so many different opinions that he was more confused than ever. In fact, he was frozen with indecision.

This situation is not unique. All too often we make mistakes by getting too much information as opposed to too little information. The more information we have, the more confusing things become.

The fact is, there is no one-to-one relationship between the amount of information you have about a market and your ability to successfully trade it! Consistent with this fact of market life are several other facts I've observed, not only in my own trading, but with other traders as well.

Consider the downside to having too much market-related information.

- *The more information you have about the markets, the more confused you'll be,* particularly if the information is contradictory. The fact is that given a plethora of information, traders will naturally try to integrate all of it into a meaningful decision. But this is no guarantee that the decision will be correct. In fact, the opinions often balance each other out and leave the trader just as confused as ever. Furthermore, even an agreement by the majority may be wrong, because it's a well-known fact that the stronger group opinions are, the more likely they are to be wrong.

- *The more information a trader has, the more likely it is that the trader will use it to justify an already established opinion or position.* Hence, the information has no value other than, perhaps, to give the trader a false sense of security.

- *The more information a trader has, the more inclined he or she will be to get caught up in the emotional tornado of trading.* Too many traders are incapable of dealing with the tick-by-tick response

5 +1.3	BL	IntTE	9.69	+.04 +2.1	IM	FF2010n	13.12	-.07 +1.4	BL	FndofAmY	25.20	-.14 +5.0	MC	MidSecs 1
3 +2.5	IL	Mgdln	9.35	+.02 +4.0	AB	FF2020n	13.07	-.11 +1.0	XC	GlobalA	35.41	+.07 +6.3	GL	SmlCapGro 1
9 +.9	BL	STGvSec	7.11	+1.1	SU	FF2030n	12.99	-.14 +.5	XC	OverseasA	19.59	+.04 +7.8	IL	SmallCo 1
										SoGenGold n15.85	+.55 -9.0	All	USGovSecs 1

of prices. Just watching the prices come across the ticker machine is enough to force them into action, action which may be totally contrary to their trading systems or methods.

- *The more information a trader has, the more likely it is that the trader will find reasons to be insecure about his or her current position.* If the information is considered expert opinion, odds are that it will have a very negative impact and may, in fact, cause the trader to make errors.

▶ Why Traders Crave Information

Given the above, we must ask why it is that traders seek information. Why is it that they cannot appreciate the value of ignorance in the markets? The simple fact of the matter is that traders have been mentally and emotionally brainwashed by Western traditions, which are themselves part and parcel of the Judaeo-Christian work ethic.

We've been taught that in order to be successful we need to work hard, we need to have as much information as possible, and we need to understand the why of things. While this may be true in some areas of life, none of it is necessarily true in stock trading. The fact is that we don't need to know the whys and wherefores of things in the markets, nor do we need to gather a wealth of information on the markets in order to make money.

This also means that we DON'T have to work hard in order to trade profitably. In fact, I've found that there is often an inverse relationship between how hard you work and how much money you make. When it comes to hard work in the markets, there is a point of diminishing returns.

▶ My Suggestions

Drawing from my many and varied experiences in the markets, I've arrived at several conclusions, all of which will, I feel, benefit

.05 +1.3	BL	IntTE	9.69	+.04 +2.1	IM	FF2010n	13.12	−.07 +1.4	BL	FndofAmY	25.20	−.14 +5.0	MC		
.03 +2.5	IL	Mgdln	9.35	+.02 +4.0	AB	FF2020n	13.07	−.11 +1.0	XC	GlobalA	35.41	+.07 +6.3	GL	SmlCapGr	
.09 +.9	BL	STGvSec	7.11	+1.1	SU	FF2030n	12.99	−.14 +.5	XC	OverseasA	19.59	+.04 +7.8	IL	SmallCo	
.10 +.3	XC									SoGenGold n	15.85	+.55 −9.0	ALL	USGovSec	

you markedly if you suffer from the information overload syndrome. Here they are:

- *Think long and hard about whether you really need a live quotation service in your home or office.* All too often I've seen good traders turn into bad traders as soon as they've added live quotes to their repertoire. Aside from being costly, these services tend to give you much more information than you need. They will encourage you to trade markets you don't need to trade or that you don't understand. They will encourage you to trade in time frames you don't want to trade (i.e., a position trader becomes a day-trader).

- *Don't get too many chart or advisory services.* In fact, think about whether you want to get a chart service at all. I've found that traders who do things the good old-fashioned way by keeping their own charts, tend to be more serious and in better touch with the technical considerations they're trying to keep track of.

- *Limit newsletters and advisory services. The simple truth is that you don't need more than one or two services.* Find a newsletter or advisory service you like, and stick with it. If you get too many opinions from too many trading advisors you'll get confused, and you won't do well.

- *Information overload from brokers.* All too many traders become sitting ducks for talkative brokers. By letting your broker jawbone you repeatedly, you'll be overloaded with all sorts of useless information. Whether consciously or unconsciously, brokers know that the more information they throw at a client, the more likely it is that the client will trade more often.

- *Compare your performance in the markets when you had a wealth of information to what it was when you were trading in relative isolation.* If my theory is correct, you'll find that you achieved your best results when you had the least amount of outside information.

- *Keep a diary in which you record the results of each trade, as well as a brief commentary about your results.* When you study them, I'm sure you'll find that those trades which were carried out most closely in line with your system served you much better than those that were interfered with as a result of information overload.

- *Make the commitment to avoid all input other than your trading system signals for a given period of time (for two months or so).* Try this experiment and see for yourself how much of a difference this practice can make. I think you'll be convinced that short-term trading in stock can be helped by a certain amount of ignorance.

▶ Additional Issues and Aspects of Discipline

These are thoughts gathered from many years of firsthand experience as a stock and futures trader. What I say may run contrary to your every fiber as a thinking person, yet you must remember that the trading game is not necessarily a game that is won by brainpower. Rather, the game is won by following your rules, letting your profits run, and closing out your losers quickly. Consider also the following thoughts:

- *Most traders are sorely lacking in discipline.* This is the single most pervasive and costly problem facing all traders. It has been the case for many years. By adding more information to his or her repertoire, the undisciplined trader will need to process even more information. The result will be less clarity and more confusion.

- *Once you've decided on a course of action based on a trading system, don't change it.* Only make a change if the system changes or your stop loss is hit. The only thing additional input can do for you is shake your discipline.

- If you're following a technical trading system, the only input you need is that which comes from your trading system.

05 +1.3	BL		IntTE	9.69	+.04 +2.1	IM	FF2010n	13.12	−.07 +1.4	BL	FndotAmY	25.20	−.14 +5.0	MC		SmiCapGr
03 +2.5	IL		Mgdin	9.35	+.02 +4.0	AB	FF2020n	13.07	−.11 +1.0	XC	GlobalA	35.41	+.07 +6.3	GL		SmallCo
09 +.9	BL		STGvSec	7.11	+.1	SU	FF2030n	12.99	−.14 +.5	XC	OverseasA	19.59	+.04 +7.8	IL		USGovSec
10 +.3	XC										SoGenGold n15.85	+.55 −9.0	AU		

When your system was designed and tested, it KNEW nothing about the news, nothing about the fundamentals and, above all, it had no emotion.

- *Remember that emotion is the chief enemy of the trader.* It is always lurking in the deep, dark, often inaccessible corners of the mind. The more you can do to beat back emotion, the more likely you are to succeed. Cutting off information is just one of the things you can do to facilitate success.

- *I encourage you to make a choice as soon as possible.* The choice is a simple one indeed. You may be a technical trader or a fundamental trader; it's a rare individual who can be both.

As a technical trader you'll have no need for the news. While there will be some news items that concern you, the majority of events, reports, etc., will be of no value to you. As a fundamental trader you will be interested in the news, reports, etc., but even a fundamental trader is still the potential victim of rumor, innuendo, worthless tips, and an entire army of emotional responses. A fundamental trader will also need to be ignorant of certain facts—specifically, facts that fall outside the realm of acceptable fundamental input.

Why do I suggest aligning yourself with one side or the other? Because the technical trader who also accepts fundamental input will often find his or her intended actions diametrically opposed to what the fundamentals are saying. This adds to confusion.

The same is true of fundamental traders. All too often the fundamentals are bullish, while the technicals are turning bearish. This poses a problem for the trader who is making decisions using both types of information.

As you can see, the value of rejecting excessive input, whether you're a technical or a fundamental trader, is significant. Take only what you need and accept no more; otherwise

5 +1.3	BL	IntTE	9.69	+.04 +2.1	IM	FF2010n	13.12	-.07 +1.4	BL	FndofAmY	25.20	-.14 +5.0	MC	MyoSecs
3 +2.5	IL	Mgdln	9.35	+.02 +4.0	AB	FF2020n	13.07	-.11 +1.0	XC	GlobalA	35.41	+.07 +6.3	GL	SmlCapGro 1
9 +.9	BL	STGvSec	7.11	+1.1	SU	FF2030n	12.99	-.14 +.5	XC	OverseasA	19.59	+.04 +7.8	IL	SmalCo 1
										SoGenGold n15.85		-.55 -9.0	AU	USGovSecs 1

you'll be overloaded with worthless information which will hurt you instead of help you.

- *Last, but by no means least, studying the behavior of highly success-ful traders* will show beyond a doubt that the discipline they exercise in not being too smart and in not second-guessing trades is one of the key ingredients, if not the single most important factor, contributing to their success. This issue of ignorance can be expressed as one of *closeness to the markets.*

While some information is necessary, too much information is destructive. In my book *Market Masters* (Dearborn Trade), I interviewed well-known traders and market analysts. The following sage advice was given to us by Robert Prechter when he was asked if a trader needs to have close contact with the markets in order to succeed:

> . . . *if you're not close enough to the markets, you lose money. If you're too close to the markets, you lose money twice as fast. You should be just as close to the markets as you need to be in order to monitor and protect your trade.*

▶ Your Choices as a Short-Term Trader

My discussion in this chapter would not be complete if it did not contain a few suggestions and comments about the choices you have as a short-term trader in stocks. It has been more than 30 years since I made my first trade in the financial markets. The longer I trade, the more I recognize and realize the incongruities and inconsistencies in the markets, as well as in the behavior of traders. I'd like to share a few of my observations in the hope that they will assist you in attaining your market goals. I believe that the clarification of your choices as a trader will facilitate your quest for success in one of the most challenging endeavors known to humankind. To achieve success, you will do well to recognize and overcome the numerous contradictions that are pervasive in the markets.

Make More by Trading Less?

Many new traders are under the mistaken impression that the amount of money they make is directly related to the amount of trading they do. While this may seem, at first glance, to be a logical conclusion, it is not necessarily a valid one. The fact is that traders are far better off having a few big winning trades than a plethora of small winners. Many successful traders agree that most of your money in short-term stock trading will be made on only a few big trades. Most of the other trades will balance themselves out between small winners, small losers, average winners, average losers, break-even trades, and commissions.

If you are not yet convinced that I'm right, it may take a few years before you agree with me. But in the end you will. If you're a floor broker who makes money by shaving a few points off trades, then it's in your best interest to trade frequently and to trade large positions for small moves. However, if you're not a pit broker you will be far better off trading less frequently but for larger moves that are often more stable. For my money, I'd rather have a few large winning trades than many smaller trades that break even or lose money in sum total.

The More Information the Better the Results

Here is another serious misconception about trading. Many traders believe that if they can acquire as much information as possible about the markets they will have a better chance of success. I believe that beyond a certain point there is an inverse correlation between how much information you have and how well you do in the markets. Too much information creates information overload. Many traders are affected adversely by too much information. Rather than educate, it obfuscates and confuses. If a trader is given too many choices, he or she can often waver or become insecure. If, however, information is limited to a few quality inputs, the end result will be a more stable source of trading decisions and, I

5 +1.3	BL	IntTE	9.69	+.04 +2.1	IM		FF2010n	13.12	-.07 +1.4	BL	FndofAmY	25.20	-.14 +5.0	MC		MyGes
3 +2.5	IL	Mgdin	9.35	+.02 +4.0	AB		FF2020n	13.07	-.11 +1.0	XC	GlobalA	35.41	+.07 +6.3	GL		SmlCapGro 1
9 +.9	BL	STGvSec	7.11	+1.1	SU		FF2030n	12.99	-.14 +.5	XC	OverseasA	19.59	+.04 +7.8	IL		SmallCo 1

believe, a profitable bottom line. I do not believe that success in trading and the amount of information you have are highly correlated. In fact, I believe that there is a point of diminishing returns as well as a point of deteriorating returns. And this holds true for everything from advisory newsletters to charts, from trading systems to timing indicators. Find a few solid inputs and stick with them if they work for you.

▶ Will a Computer Help You Trade Better?

While I am not old-fashioned, I do believe that the need for computers has been overstated and overrated. Although they are certainly timesaving tools with fabulous capabilities, computers can also create unnecessary dependencies. The computer industry has done a splendid job selling computers to the world. Although I can appreciate the value of a computer in stock and futures trading, I am not at all convinced that a computer will help you trade better. After all, a computer is only a tool. It does what you tell it to do. In the hands of a trader who is determined to break the rules, a computer will only facilitate the process, thereby resulting in more losses as opposed to better performance. I believe that traders can do quite well without the use of a computer. The "good old-fashioned way" of keeping charts by hand and doing calculations by hand is still well worthwhile. While I appreciate the value of a computer in research, trading and information storage, I do not feel that the mere use of a computer will ensure your success as a trader. A computer is like a car. A bad driver can't become a good driver by getting a new car. Anyone who has a self-destructive side will eventually shoot himself or herself unless they make substantive changes in their behavior. While a computer can help you make these changes, nothing will happen unless YOU change first.

Electronic trading of stocks is indeed a wonderful thing. Your trades are executed quickly, and you pay lower commissions than if you deal with a broker. On the other hand, having access to fast price fills and instant feedback can cause some individuals to become addicted to trading. A computer can be a very helpful tool if you do not allow yourself to become addicted to short-term trading.

▶ Will a System Help You Trade Better?

A system can help you trade better but it won't do so unless you meet some very important minimum requirements. First, you must have sufficient capital to trade the system you have selected. A fantastic system that cannot be traded due to insufficient capital is like a work of art locked in a vault. It will never be appreciated. The second requirement is (as always) discipline. The best trading system in the world will lose money if traded by an undisciplined, inconsistent, or inexperienced trader. And the third requirement is that you have the tools necessary to follow the system. Unless all of the above requirements have been met, you will not be successful with a trading system no matter how good the system may be. As you can see, a trading system can't help you unless you're ready for the help.

▶ Do Commissions Represent Quality of Service?

This is not always true. I agree that commissions should be reasonable. But remember that the cost of commissions is a two-edged sword. For the new trader, or for the trader who requires guidance and "hand-holding," discount commissions may not be the best way to go. In fact, electronic trading may not be the best way to go, either. The majority of discount commission houses, whether on- or offline, will not take the time to assist new traders. At super discount prices, they can't afford to take time with you. A new trader could be spared from making some costly mistakes if he or she had a broker who could provide input about such simple things as the best order to use, or how to place a spread order, or when to place an order.

For the experienced trader who wants no input, a discount broker may be best as long as the quality of service (i.e., price fills and timely reporting back of fills) is acceptable. If this is not the case, it might be better to pay a little more to get better service. And for the trader who is neither a novice nor a veteran, a higher commission than discount might be beneficial, because such commissions nowadays come with many perks, such as free subscriptions, books, charts, quotations, and market reports.

On the other side of the coin are expensive commissions. Do they reflect a better product in terms of advice or research? I don't think so. As an independent trader who uses my methods or those you have developed on your own, you do not need broker input or research. Such research may, in fact, be detrimental to your success.

▶ Traders Want to Succeed but . . . Why Don't They Act Like It?

This is perhaps the most glaring inconsistency I have seen in my 30-plus years as a trader, market analyst, and writer. I agree that short-term trading in stocks and futures is perhaps the most difficult thing anyone can attempt in the field of trading or investing. Many aspiring traders have stepped up to the bat, only to strike out quickly. Most traders who fail at trading are reasonably intelligent (perhaps too intelligent) people who have a sincere desire to succeed. However, that desire often supercedes their willingness to work hard at the skill and profession of short-term stock trading. Too many would-be traders believe that the stock market is like a treasure chest waiting to be opened. They erroneously believe that because they have been successful in business or in their profession it is a foregone conclusion that success in trading is a *fait accompli*. They soon find out that they couldn't be more wrong! Successful short-term trading in stocks requires a particular type of knowledge as well as a rigorous type of self-discipline. Few, if any of us are born with the knowledge or discipline necessary to succeed at the game. Therefore, both must be learned. The learning process takes time, money, persistence, and a good teacher. Yes, it can be learned from books; however, it will take more time. The knowledge to trade successfully doesn't fall out of a magazine.

In today's age of "instantism" people are obsessed with the desire for immediate success. They are constantly barraged by junk mail, e-mail and television commercials touting products, services, and new businesses that promise quick and fantastic results. It's no wonder that people feel pressured to achieve instant results from their stock trading. In short, we have been brainwashed and hyped into believing that we need to do very little work in order to achieve success in trading. This is not the case. Although the concepts and methods of short-term stock trading may be simple and easy to understand, they require practice and discipline. The methods may not take long to learn, but they must be applied with consistency. Self-discipline, consistency, persistence, and patience are not inherent human qualities. They must be learned. As you can see, there are several levels of learning and many things to learn. Few traders I have met are willing to make the effort required to learn the game. They want success handed to them on a silver platter. It won't happen.

CHAPTER

11

30 Tools to
Build Profits

 If you believe that a good trading system is a surefire ticket to profits, you are WRONG!

If you think that good traders are "born" with their skills, you are WRONG!

If you believe that you can win at the market without the right tools, you are WRONG!

Spend some time studying my list of 30 tools to help you achieve profits. As discussed in the last chapter, effective trader discipline and a

.05	+1.3	BL		IntTE	9.69	+.04	+2.1	IM		FF2010 n	13.12	-.07	+1.4	BL		FndotAmY	25.20	-.14	+5.0	MC		MidSecs
.03	+2.5	IL		Mgdln	9.35	+.02	+4.0	AB		FF2020 n	13.07	-.11	+1.0	XC		GlobalA	35.41	+.07	+6.3	GL		SmlCapGr
.09	+.9	BL		STGvSec	7.11		+1.1	SU		FF2030 n	12.99	-.14	+.5	XC		OverseasA	19.59	+.04	+7.8	IL		SmallCo
.10	+.3	XC														SoGenGold n	15.85	+.55	-9.0	ALL		USGovSec

healthy psychological structure are the quintessential underpinnings of profitable trading. My list is designed to help you overcome the all too common factors that limit trader and investor success. Yes, you can gloss over this chapter. Yes, you can skip this chapter entirely. If, however, you are like most traders, you will come back to this chapter after you have suffered a series of losses. The best way to help minimize those losses or eliminate the majority of them is to take some preventative measures now.

Here are my suggestions and observations.

1. Understand Why You Trade Stocks.

The successful trader has a clear and concise goal. *This goal is not primarily to beat the market, nor is it to become skillful for the sake of skill alone.*

The profit-making trader is, first and foremost, interested in *profits*. It matters little how these profits are achieved as long as they are attained legally, morally and ethically. In fact, to far too many traders, ethics and morals are of little importance as long as profits are obtained legally. And there are even those who don't concern themselves with the legalities, either.

Yes, traders are a mercenary lot. If you trade stocks for the enjoyment, the thrill, or the challenge, then your motives are dead wrong.

If you trade for any reason other than to make money, you are best advised to quit now or change your goal.

2. Most Traders Are Losers in the Markets.

As you know well enough from your own trading experiences, there is no surefire or simple road to success in the markets unless you have foolproof inside information and unless you use that information correctly. With so many books, systems, and methods to choose from, it would seem that success is readily obtainable. But it is NOT!

5 +1.3	BL	IntTE	9.69	+.04 +2.1	IM		FF2010n	13.12	-.07 +1.4	BL	FndofAmY	25.20	-.14 +5.0	MC		SmiCapGro	1
3 +2.5	IL	Mgdln	9.35	+.02 +4.0	AB		FF2020n	13.07	-.11 +1.0	XC	GlobalA	35.41	+.07 +6.3	GL		SmallCo	1
9 +.9	BL	STGvSec	7.11	+1.1	SU		FF2030n	12.99	-.14 +.5	XC	OverseasA	19.59	+.04 +7.8	IL		USGovSecs	1

Most traders are losers in the markets. And the shorter term their time frame of trading is, the more likely they are to be losers. On the other hand, investors who buy and hold stocks for many years have often made vast sums of money, provided they have picked the correct stocks and/or mutual funds. But the key here is buy the right stocks and hold them. Does this mean that there is no room for the short-term trader? Not at all! It simply means that the short-term trader will need to be more disciplined, more aggressive, and more willing to trade a larger number of shares in order to compensate for the fact that shorter-term trades yield smaller profits than long-term investments.

What you ultimately develop through your efforts to learn stock trading will be an individual, tailor-made approach designed specifically to suit your purposes. Whether you end up with a purely mechanical approach, based on the research of others, or a primarily subjective approach, based on your own interpretations and studies, the fact remains that the ultimate decision making is yours and yours alone.

Regardless of what you select as your methodology or how you select it, there are some common threads that weave through the fabric of every successful approach to stock (and commodity) trading. *These common aspects influence and regulate the success or failure of virtually every trader.*

3. WEAKEST LINK IN THE CHAIN: THE TRADER.

While it may be true that some individuals achieve success by breaking all the rules, it is also true that such individuals are clearly in the minority and that their success is the exception, rather than the rule. Unless you are blessed with fantastic luck, you will need to achieve success in the markets the good old-fashioned way: You will have to earn it.

The only way to earn lasting success is through the diligent and disciplined application of specific techniques and methods, *few of which are directly related to systems, and most of which are clearly the function of attitudes, psychology, and discipline.*

You may not want to hear this, but the fact is that it matters little what system or systems you use, how tremendous their hypothetical performance may be, or how well others may have done with these systems. What ultimately matters is how you *apply* the systems, and the consistency with which you can put the techniques into operation.

A great trading system when used by an undisciplined trader is a LOSING system.

A poor trading system when used a disciplined trader can be a MONEY-MAKER.

The human being is not a computer—he or she cannot achieve the same level of perfection that may be required to implement a trading system by the rules under which it was tested. The degree of error is often significant and can cause a system that is profitable in back-testing to be a LOSER in real time. What makes the difference is the way the trader uses (or abuses) the system. And from what we know of traders, they abuse systems more often than they use them.

Real-time market conditions often deteriorate the performance of most systems. In fact, no system based on hypothetical or computer-simulated or tested results can be taken as worthwhile unless the results can be replicated with reasonable similarity in real time.

4. FOCUS ON THE TRADER AND NOT THE SYSTEM!

Don't waste your time trying to perfect the ideal trading system if you don't have the discipline and ability to use that system. Having the "perfect" trading system but not knowing how to use it is like dreaming of the "perfect" lover you will never meet or, what's worse, actually finding that lover but not knowing what to do!

The steps to trading success do not rest exclusively, or for that matter heavily, upon selection of a system. Although we know that the selection of a trading system or method is important, its value has been overrated, particularly by those with a vested interest in selling you systems, books, seminars, or trading courses.

In order to achieve success you MUST follow most, if not all, of the time-tested rules of profitable trading. There is NO OTHER WAY TO MAKE MONEY AND KEEP IT other than by sheer dumb luck—and that doesn't happen too often!

5. Find or Develop a Trading System that Has a Real-Time Record.

A real-time record (or computer-tested record) is one of 60 percent or more winning trades, with a ratio of approximately 2 to 1 in terms of dollars made versus dollars lost per trade (including commissions and slippage as losses). In the absence of real-time results, computer results are acceptable, provided you've made provisions for their limitations. Though the performance figures I gave you need not be replicated exactly, attempt to get close. All you want in a system is a larger average profit than the average loss, a profitable bottom line that is worthwhile, and reasonably good historical accuracy. You want a vehicle that will get you from point A to point B safely, efficiently, and perhaps even enjoyably.

You can get your trading advice from an advisory service, hotline, or newsletter, but before you follow any of these services with real money, track their performance for a few months (at least) and/or study how they performed in different market conditions.

Remember that almost anyone can make money in a big bull market. It's the bear market and the choppy market that separate good systems and services from bad ones.

There are many systems, methods, and indicators that can get you where you're going—and you don't have to pay a system seller big bucks to get them.

6. The System(s) You Find or Develop Should Be Consistent with Your Time Limitations or Availability.

This is true with or without a computer system. If the signals are generated by an advisory service, then make certain you have

.05 +1.3	BL	IntTE	9.69	+.04 +2.1	IM	FF2010n	13.12	–.07 +1.4	BL	FndofAmY	25.20	–.14 +5.0	MC	MgSecs
.03 +2.5	IL	Mgdln	9.35	+.02 +4.0	AB	FF2020n	13.07	–.11 +1.0	XC	GlobalA	35.41	+.07 +6.3	GL	SmlCapGr
.09 +.9	BL	STGvSec	7.11	+1.1	SU	FF2030n	12.99	–.14 +5	XC	OverseasA	19.59	+.04 +7.8	IL	SmallCo
.10 +.3	XC									SoGenGold n15.85	+.55 –9.0	AL	USGovSec

familiarized yourself with the basics of the system, its trading approach, and other details of the system as described earlier in the text. There are thousands of investors who want to be day traders or short-term traders, but they are unwilling to make the time commitment required to achieve success. Your system must be compatible with your ability to implement it.

I am ever amused by the large number of people I meet who tell me they want to be day traders but who have full-time jobs during the day. While there are a few day trading methods that do not require constant attention and live price quotations, the majority of day trading techniques and systems need to be monitored all day. What is it about people that makes them think they can day trade and work full-time during the day? It's called being out of touch with reality!

Be honest with yourself. Never try to do in the market what you haven't the time, skill, education, or equipment to do. Trying to win at a game you can't play with a full deck is to be a loser before you begin! You say that you "know all this." Think about it. Do you really "know all this," or are you attempting to do something you really can't do?

7. START WITH SUFFICIENT RISK CAPITAL.

What also amazes me is the number of people who think they can be successful by starting with a few hundred dollars. In part, the media hype in recent years is responsible for that lie. Yes, you CAN begin to invest with only a few dollars if you buy mutual funds. Yes, you CAN begin to trade with only a few hundred dollars, but it's going to be difficult. Why tilt the odds against yourself by trying to start on a shoestring? If you begin with only a few hundred dollars you'll be out of the game after only a few losses.

Be certain that your risk capital is truly risk capital and not funds upon which you are otherwise counting for some future purpose. Trading with "scared money" is a surefire invitation to losses.

8. Develop and Formulate Your Goals and Philosophy.

What? What the heck does philosophy have to do with making money in the markets? Are the two compatible? Indeed they are. Your perceptions of trading, your expectations, your goals, and your market orientation (i.e., long-term, short-term) are all factors that contribute either to success or failure. It's really that simple. You can't get to your goal unless you have one. And you can't get to a goal unless you have a vehicle to get you there. For some absurd reason, newcomers (and even experienced traders) think they can make money in the markets without having a plan, goals, and methods. They would never approach a "real business" venture in the same way, yet they think they can be profitable as traders without these prerequisites. This belief is absurd and bound to get them into trouble. *Have a goal. Have a method. Have a philosophy or you will lose.*

9. Plan and Execute.

Never trade on a whim.
- Don't "take shot" on a trade.
- Don't take a "gamble" on a trade.
- Don't buy or sell because a stock "looks like" it "wants" to go up or down!
- Don't follow a "hunch," feeling, or educated guess. These are all BS (excuse me) excuses for being impulsive, unsystematic, undisciplined, and in poor self-control.

These are all losing behaviors. They will get you into trouble.

Work from a trading plan, system, or method EVERY time you trade so you will avoid the temptation of making spur-of-the-moment decisions that are not based on any system or method you are using.

If you lose money on a trade made by your system, you'll know that the system didn't work that time. If you lose money by trading on a whim, a rumor, a feeling, or a hunch, you have learned nothing!

.05	+1.3	BL	InTE	9.69	+.04	+2.1	IM	FF2010n	13.12	-.07	+1.4	BL	FndofAmY	25.20	-.14	+5.0	MC	MyBotS
.03	+2.5	IL	Mgdin	9.35	+.02	+4.0	AB	FF2020n	13.07	-.11	+1.0	XC	GlobalA	35.41	+.07	+6.3	GL	SmlCapGr
.09	+.9	BL	STGvSec	7.11		+1.1	SU	FF2030n	12.99	-.14	+.5	XC	OverseasA	19.59	+.04	+7.8	IL	SmallCo
.10	+.3	XC											SoGenGoldn15.85		+.55	-9.0	AU	USGovSec

10. BE AN ISOLATIONIST.

There is great value in being a loner when it comes to speculation and trading. You don't necessarily want anyone else's input. You don't necessarily want anyone else's opinions. As time goes on, as the lessons you learn begin to accumulate, you will realize that your own good opinion is just as valuable, perhaps more so, than the opinions of any others—experts or novices.

Think about how often the "experts" have been wrong. Do you really need their advice? Is there a way you can use expert opinions to your advantage? Yes, there is. You can listen for ideas but not for specific trades. *Experts can do an excellent job of telling you when to get into a stock but they usually aren't there to tell you when to get out or how much to risk.*

11. MAKE A COMMITMENT; TAKE THE PLUNGE!

Make a commitment to trading. The commitment should consist of rules, organizational procedures, goals, and expectations. Delineate these carefully, with consideration and forethought. By making your plans, you will avoid costly errors that are not consistent with your plans. There are many would-be traders who make no plans but plunge recklessly into the waters, only to drown after a few trades. Before you jump into the waters, make sure you have your plans set and ready to put into action.

12. DON'T HESITATE!

Don't hesitate for even a moment once your trading decision has been made (whether the decision is to get into or out of a trade). It matters not whether you are taking a profit or closing out a loss. As soon as you have a clear-cut signal, based on your system or method, don't hesitate. Act as soon as your system says you must act—no sooner, no later.

With today's ease of order entry you can have your trades executed online in a matter of seconds. Remember that there are

5 +1.3	BL	IntTE	9.69	+.04 +2.1	IM		FF2010 n	13.12	-.07 +1.4	BL		FndofAmY	25.20	-.14 +5.0	MC		MdySecs
3 +2.5	IL	Mgdln	9.35	+.02 +4.0	AB		FF2020 n	13.07	-.11 +1.0	XC		GlobalA	35.41	+.07 +6.3	GL		SmlCapGro 1
9 +.9	BL	STGvSec	7.11	+.1	SU		FF2030 n	12.99	-.14 +.5	XC		OverseasA	19.59	+.04 +7.8	IL		SmallCo 1
	XC											SoGenGold n	15.85	-.55 -9.0	ALL		USGovSecs 1

thousands of other traders out there competing with you. If you're a day trader, speed of order execution is one of the most important things. Why lose the edge by hesitating once you have a trading signal?

13. LIMIT RISK/PRESERVE CAPITAL.

The best way to limit risk is to trade only in three to six stocks at once and to avoid trading stocks that are too volatile for your account size. Once you have decided to limit risk to a certain dollar amount or by using a specific technique, make certain to take your losses as soon as they should be taken. Do this on time—not too soon, not too late! Most of the biggest losses I have taken in my years as a trader have resulted from failing to take a loss when it was small and manageable. Losses rarely get better if you wait.

14. DON'T ANTICIPATE SIGNALS AND TRADES.

Many traders go astray when they anticipate signals from their trading system. The trading system is your traffic light. The traffic is always heavy. Stop on the red, go on the green, and be cautious on yellow. If you anticipate trading signals from your system, you might as well not have a system at all.

I understand that this may run contrary to your self-concept as a "thinking" individual. We all want to feel that we are part of the decision-making process; that we have valuable input and experience to offer; that we can use our intellect to make money. We can! *But if you have developed a system, all of the thought and brains and experience have already gone into the system. So use it!*

15. THE MARKET IS YOUR MASTER, YOU ARE ITS SLAVE.

Like it or not, you cannot tell the market what to do. It will always do what it wants, and it is your job to figure out what it is doing. You must follow the market through its many twists and turns. If it is zigging and zagging, then you must zig and zag. If it is trending

.05 +1.3	BL	InfTE	9.69	+.04 +2.1	IM	FF2010n	13.12	-.07 +1.4	BL	FndofAmY	25.20	-.14 +5.0	MC	MuySecs	
.03 +2.5	IL	Mgdln	9.35	+.02 +4.0	AB	FF2020n	13.07	-.11 +1.0	XC	GlobalA	35.41	+.07 +6.3	GL	SmiCapGr
.09 +.9	BL	STGvSec	7.11	+1.1	SU	FF2030n	12.99	-.14 +.5	XC	OverseasA	19.59	+.04 +7.8	IL	SmallCo
.10 +.3	XC									SoGenGold n15.85		+.55 -9.0	ALL	USGovSec

higher, you must trade from the long side. If it is trending lower, you must trade from the short side.

It may be instructive for you to review, from time to time, which side of the market most of your trades were on. If you find that you have been bucking the trend of the market or of a given stock, then you must review your system or your discipline. One of the two (perhaps both) are not functioning properly. Many traders have gone astray by failing to follow the market, thinking that it is their job to forecast stock trends. The job of the trader is to follow, not to forecast. *Leave forecasting to economists—you're a trader, not an economist.*

16. DO YOUR HOMEWORK.

Whether you use a computer or pen and pencil, or whether you are a novice or a seasoned trader, you must keep your research current. Markets move so fast these days that there is precious little time to update your trading signals once a move has occurred. You must be there at the very inception of a move or shortly thereafter. Otherwise you will have difficulty getting aboard for the bigger move. The only way to do this is to keep your homework up-to-date. If you have a computer it may be easier. You can program your computer so it will automatically update your signals or system every day at a given time. Regardless, discipline is always involved and you must keep current.

17. AVOID EMOTION—BE A "VULCAN."

You need to be emotionless like Mr. Spock of Star Trek. The greatest friend of the trader is the emotion of others, but your own emotions can be among your worst enemies. When trading, emotions must be under control—impulsive acts are to be strictly avoided. Emotions and their consequences can be exceptionally dangerous to the speculator because they can result in unwarranted actions. I could write an entire book on this topic (in fact, I have). Yes, I know

5 +1.3	BL		IntTE	9.69	+.04 +2.1	IM		FF2010n	13.12	–.07 +1.4	BL		FndofAmY	25.20	–.14 +5.0	MC		MuySecs
3 +2.5	IL		Mgdln	9.35	+.02 +4.0	AB		FF2020n	13.07	–.11 +1.0	XC		GlobalA	35.41	+.07 +6.3	GL		SmlCapGro 1
9 +.9	BL		STGvSec	7.11	+1.1	SU		FF2030n	12.99	–.14 +5	XC		OverseasA	19.59	+.04 +7.8	IL		SmallCo

you've heard this rule hundreds of times, but if you are still acting impulsively, you haven't learned the rule. It's a simple rule but it's very difficult to put into action.

18. Assume Full Responsibility for All Your Trading Actions.

Accepting that you alone are responsible for the outcome of your trading is a major step toward achieving success. Many traders are unaware that they put a psychological barrier between the actions they take and the results of those actions. They try to blame other people, the market, or anything that will remove the focus of responsibility from themselves. Becoming rigorously honest and "owning" your actions will lead to consistency and success in the markets. *If you ever find yourself blaming your broker, your partner, the market, your trading advisor, or anyone but yourself, you are not learning anything from your mistakes. You must own all your losses as well as your profits.*

19. Hope and Fear Have NO PLACE in Your Trading Plan.

Both attitudes turn a trader into a passive player. When you hope a position will go your way or fear that it will go against you, you abandon your ability to think and take action. Hope and fear are similar and will produce behavior that is paralyzing for the trader. Inability to respond to trading signals will destroy a trader's confidence and lead to substantial losses.

20. Avoid Overconfidence—It Will Breed Complacency.

Have you ever noticed that traders who have a string of big winning trades tend to follow up with a big loss that often takes back all of their profits? Why does this happen? The emotional "high" of achieving success in the market can lead to such a feeling of satisfaction that one actually becomes lazy. The market is oblivious to your experience of success or failure and therefore demands that you always pay attention when you are involved. Allowing your judgment to be impaired by any emotional extreme will precipitate a potential trading disaster.

21. MONITOR YOUR PERFORMANCE AND PAY ATTENTION TO RESULTS.

The rapidity of change in today's markets is unlike that of any time in history. The opportunity for a trader to receive constant and instantaneous feedback is always present. How much and how often a trader wants to observe this fact and learn from his or her actions is another question. It has been said that trading the markets is similar to getting a report card every day. The ability to take advantage of this feedback and learn from it will lead to increased confidence and success in the markets.

22. DEVELOP POSITIVE RELATIONSHIPS.

People influence how we look at the world and how we think about ourselves. Friends often act as a mirror of our own reality. Consequently, it is important to surround yourself with people who have a positive sense of themselves. If you associate with people who complain, blame, or whose energy is low, you will be influenced by their behavior. Moods are contagious. If you surround yourself with negative people, you will eventually become negative. As a trader, it is critical to be aware of the company you keep and to be with those who maintain a positive and winning attitude.

23. DON'T TRADE ON TIPS, SURE THINGS, OR INSIDE INFORMATION.

The temptation in all of us is to find the easy way. But you know the easy way is rarely the best way. There will always be lottery winners, but your odds of winning any lottery are slim. Therefore, avoid the temptation of taking tips, following inside information, listening to the opinions of other traders, or believing that the person you are listening to or talking to knows more than you do. Sometimes they do, but most of the time they don't. Collective

opinions are, of course, helpful in the case of contrary-opinion studies, but individual opinions or tips are basically useless to the trader.

24. When You Make Money, Take Some of It Away from the Market.

When you have been doing well, remember to systematically
remove money from your account. Whether you do this on a profitable trade basis or on a time basis (i.e., daily, weekly, monthly) is
not important. What is important is that you do it. Traders have winning and losing periods. During the winning times, profits will accumulate rapidly, and before you know it you may become impressed
with your success. You will examine ways to expand your trading in
view of your tremendous profits. You will look at how much money
there is in your account and be tempted to trade larger positions.

While there will be a time for this, it is usually not right to do
so when you are feeling euphoric about your performance. One
way to reduce euphoria and put profits away for a rainy day is by
having a systematic method of withdrawing profits.

25. Develop Winning Attitudes and Behaviors.

You can do this by reading the writings of the great traders. Spend
more time developing yourself than you do developing your systems. The key variable in the trading-success equation is the trader
and not the system. I maintain that a good trader can make virtually any system work.

26. "The Trend Is Your Friend."

This old expression is known to all, but used by few. Whether you
allow the major trend to filter signals from your system as the final
deciding factor, or whether you use a system that is based entirely
on trend-following principles, always be cautious when your
trades are not consistent with the existing trend. Naturally, there
will be times when your signals are against the trend. There will be
times when the trend is apt to change. However, you should

always be careful about trades and signals against the trend because they will most often be wrong.

27. Don't Try to Trade Too Many Stocks at the Same Time.

There are many different stocks, but most of them move together. There are only a few major industry groups. Establish a portfolio of stocks you are following and trade within that group.

28. Don't Take the Markets Home with You.

Trading can be an all-consuming business and whether you are trading well or not, it is advisable to get into the habit of leaving the markets at the office. Do not carry the effects of your trading into other aspects of your life. If you are trading well, you may become complacent in areas where you need to work. Conversely, trading poorly can often lead you to feel depressed and not motivated to take care of other concerns in your life. Try to keep work separate from other areas and reserve time to take vacations and get away from the trading environment.

29. Don't Lose Sight of Your Goals.

Your goal in trading is to make money. There is no goal greater than this in trading. Though there may be other benefits such as self-satisfaction, the thrill of trading, and the sublimation of hostility and competitive instincts, these are all secondary. If you seek revenge against the market or other traders, if you wish merely to compete for the sake of competition or to trade only for the thrill of trading, then the primary goal of speculation will be lost—and so will your money!

30. Keep Good Records.

You will be amazed at how much you can learn by looking over the history of your trades. Every time you trade, jot down why you made the trade and its outcome. Compare what you did with what your system or method told you to do. If there are discrepancies, it means you have a lot of soul-searching to do. Chances are, you will be a net loser if there are too many times that you failed to follow your signals.

▶ It's Your Decision—Succeed or Fail

Though some rules may be more important to you than others, I know that at one time or another, all of these will be important to all traders. The best way to employ these rules in your trading program is to study them, to keep them at your disposal, and to review them regularly. They will help keep you honest with yourself and on the right track.

Perhaps one of the greatest errors a speculator can commit is self-deception. The markets are brutal and the pain of losses is omnipresent. No trader or speculator is immune to losses. What ultimately separates the winners from the losers is the ability to be honest with oneself. From this rare quality arises clear perception. From a clear perception of reality comes the ability to use only what is effective and to discard all that is not.

So You Want to Strengthen Your Discipline?

I've been trading the markets only since 1968. Maybe I've learned something. Perhaps you believe what I've told you. If you do believe me and if you want to make some changes for the good, you may want to read and internalize what follows.

▶ Maximizing Profits, Minimizing Losses

Whether you seek to excel as writer, trader, doctor, or investor, you will rarely achieve your goals through luck. You will most often arrive at your destination through the application of time-tested rules applied consistently, repeatedly, diligently and with discipline. I will share with you an in-depth examination of trading discipline, its definition, intricacies, and application. Most traders do not understand the meaning of discipline, and as a result discipline has become a perennial topic of conversation among traders.

▶ Defining Trading Discipline

One of the main reasons so many traders find it difficult to master discipline is that they have not first defined it. For many traders discipline is illusory. They chase phantoms that approach the true substance of discipline, but fail to catch them because they never materialize with sufficient clarity. So let us begin with a working definition of trading discipline.

Trading Discipline

Acting in complete accordance with the signals generated by a trading system, method, or procedure, and with the risk management rules that accompany that system, method, or procedure.

Discipline is a matter of individuality. Because personalities and needs vary from one individual to another, an effort that requires discipline and self-control for one person requires virtually no effort for another. Tasks achieved with considerable effort by some traders are completed in virtually automatic fashion by others. What poses a chronic problem for some traders has never been, and will probably never be, a problem for other traders.

Being disciplined in following a trading system is useless if:

- One does not have the discipline to keep his/her trading system up-to-date.
- One does not have the discipline to follow sound risk management.

As you can see, trading discipline is multifaceted and interdependent. There are layers and levels of discipline, all of which interact to produce positive or negative results.

▶ The Three Levels of Trading Discipline

I. *Preparation and Planning*

If a trader is to trade a system, the system must be maintained in working order. You must do your homework by keeping your work up-to-date and accurate if it is to serve you well with valid trading signals.

- Have someone else do it for you. There are many individuals who enjoy following procedures and plans. Hire one of them to do the work for you if you cannot or prefer not to do it on your own and with consistency.
- Get your trading signals from an advisory service or trading advisor. As simple as these procedures may be, there are thousands of traders who cannot follow them. They become especially difficult for some traders to follow when they are losing money. That's when the real test comes. By having someone else do this for you, you will avoid failing at this level.
- Be on the lookout for unconscious error in generating your signals when you are in a losing streak. You can easily make mistakes that you are not even aware of but which are the result of a negative attitude.

II. *Implementation*

Most traders find this to be the single most difficult aspect of discipline. While they have no trouble updating their trading systems, they have great difficulty implementing them. The problem is so pervasive that several books could be written on this topic alone. Because each individual has his/her own personal experience of what creates the fear, it must be dealt with on an individual basis.

.05	+1.3	BL	IntTE	9.69	+.04	+2.1	IM	FF2010n	13.12	−.07	+1.4	BL	FndofAmY	25.20	−.14	+5.0	MC	MtgSecs	
.03	+2.5	IL	Mgdln	9.35	+.02	+4.0	AB	FF2020n	13.07	−.11	+1.0	XC	GlobalA	35.41	+.07	+6.3	GL	SmlCapGr
.09	+.9	BL	STGvSec	7.11		+1.1	SU	FF2030n	12.99	−.14	+.5	XC	OverseasA	19.59	+.04	+7.8	IL	SmallCo
.10	+.3	XC											SoGenGold n15.86		+.55	−9.0	ALL	USGovSec

FEAR OF LOSSES

Fear of losses is a conscious fear. Traders will not take action when they are afraid of losing money. It's that simple. And fear can escalate with each loss until it reaches the point of complete withdrawal. This is a normal reaction to losses. If you touch a hot stove and you get burned, you will be disinclined to touch it again.

But if the stove is hot at times and not hot at others, you will never know when to touch it. If opening the door of the oven allows you to put your hand in and take money out, the dilemma is even more anxiety-provoking. It presents the classic "approach-avoidance" situation, which is one of the most difficult to cope with.

Laboratory animals in this situation are locked into inconsistent and neurotic behaviors for many years. It is the fact that you do not know when the reward's coming that makes this problem so severe.

FEAR OF PROFIT

There are many traders who would be very uncomfortable if they were successful. These are individuals who fear their own impulses. In most cases they have such low self-esteem that they refuse to accept the fact that they can be winners. Why do they continue to play the game? They do so because they have not yet come to grips with their unconscious desire to avoid winning. They are essentially normal individuals, yet they know down deep that nothing they have ever done in their lives has been a complete victory—that nothing they have ever done has been thoroughly enjoyed. In such cases, lack of discipline is deep-rooted and must be treated by a mental-health professional although it can be remedied in more mechanical ways.

HOW TO OVERCOME THE SHY TRIGGER FINGER

- *Have someone else pull the trigger for you.* The preferred choice is a person who is detached, a person who does not have a vested interest in your trading.

- *Develop a system of checks and balances.* Cross-check your system with another trader whose trading is similar to the way you trade. By monitoring the same trading signals, you can keep each other honest.

III. Risk Management

This is by far the most mismanaged area of trading. It is the area responsible for small losses turning into large losses, or for potentially large profits being picked off the vine prematurely as small profits. Most traders I have talked to readily admit that their largest losing trades have most often been trades that could have been closed out as small losers according to their trading system but were left too long.

The ability to close out losers promptly and to ride winners is by far the most important of all trading disciplines. More traders have lost more money by riding losers than by picking bad trades that were closed out as small losses. But how to close out those losers? That is the big question. Again, the answer is simple. If you cannot close out those losers when you have to, get someone to do it for you. Along these lines, I have several suggestions:

- If your system uses a stop-loss immediately upon entering a position, then enter your stop-loss immediately as well. If the stop stays the same for the duration of the trade, enter an open order (good until canceled).
- If your system uses a trailing stop-loss, make certain you enter the trailing stop-loss each time it needs to be changed.
- To stay honest with your system and yourself, have another individual monitor your system(s) and evaluate your discipline accordingly.
- Use a checklist. Check off each item as it is completed.

How to Determine What Is Right for You

Goals and needs go hand in hand. To determine exactly how your trading discipline can be improved, several questions must first be answered.

I. Do You Need to Improve Your Discipline?

- A simple way to find the answer to this question is to look at your performance.
- Is it significantly different from the ideal performance of your system or method?
- Are you losing money when your system says you should be making money?
- Have the markets acted as you expected?
- Have you made money from your expectations? If you are not performing as your system would ideally dictate, and if you are not profiting from your signals and/or projections, it is likely that your discipline is at fault. If however, you are satisfied with your profits and are trading in accordance with your plans and system, no changes in discipline are indicated at this time.

II. Isolate the Source of Your Losses

- Determine the reason(s) for your losses. This means that each loss must be examined in detail.
- Determine the cause of each loss. Causes can fall into many different categories. They can be due to emotion, errors, disorganization, lack of sufficient margin, and a host of other variables. You will not be able to change the cause until you have identified it.

III. Be Specific

- When you investigate the cause of each loss, do so in considerable detail.
- Retrace all your steps, from the original technical signal to the actual liquidation of the trade.
- Be as specific as possible in tracking down the reason(s) for each losing trade.

IV. KEEP A DIARY

- A diary of your trading should be kept to help determine the quality of your discipline, or lack thereof. By retracing your steps you may find clues to your difficulty. Record the following:
  - Date, time, and price trade was entered.
  - Reason(s) for entry (be specific).
  - Date, time, and price trade was closed out.
  - Reason(s) for exit (be specific).
  - Any thoughts, feelings, special situations, problems, or events that transpired directly before or after you entered or exited the trade. (Frequently, the mere act of keeping a diary will alert you to potential or actual problems with discipline.)
- The best time to write in your diary is when you enter or exit a given trade. If you are too busy, however, then update your diary at the end of the trading day.
- I maintain that a diary is extremely important in tracking discipline. Every trader should keep a diary, whether he or she is making or losing money. A diary can be the source of much important information.

V. DO NOT RULE ANYTHING OUT

- When you are looking for answers, consider everything. Something as simple as talking to the wrong people can be the source of your lack of discipline.

VI. LOOK FOR PATTERNS

- Study your behavior in detail and watch for patterns and repertoire.
- Determine what events or feelings come immediately before and immediately after your lack of discipline.

▶ A Few Closing Thoughts About Discipline

So what is the "bottom line" of the trading discipline issue? There are several points that deserve mention.

Trading Discipline Can Be Learned

Discipline of any kind is NOT innate. We learn it from exposure to various learning experiences, most of which come from our parents and teachers. While it is true that some people appear to be more organized than others, I emphasize that organization and discipline are not one and the same. There are many highly organized traders who have not yet mastered the finer points of discipline.

Trading Discipline Is by Far the Weakest Link in the Trading Chain

Without discipline, virtually nothing is possible. Any trader who feels that he or she can achieve lasting success without trading discipline is living a lie. Those who fail to develop the skills that are part and parcel of trading discipline are doomed to failure. Any trader who refuses to accept the importance of discipline in the three areas I've outlined previously is destined to fail repeatedly. Anyone who has not overcome the problems that arise as a function of poor discipline will never be successful, other than through luck.

Trading Discipline Is at Least as Important as Your Trading System

You must find ways to make the two work together for you. A system without discipline is like a ship without a rudder—it cannot be guided through the treacherous waters safely. It will be dashed upon the rocks when seas are stormy.

Trading Discipline Should be Your Priority

Place it number one on your list, even ahead of having an effective trading system. Learn discipline first by applying some of the suggestions I have given you. Talk to expert traders, observe the habits of successful traders, study your losing trades, find out where you went wrong each time you take a loss and, above all, always distinguish between losses you took as a function of poor discipline, and losses you took in following a system.

Loss resulting from following a system is acceptable and you will learn from it. The other type of loss is unacceptable and you will not grow unless you understand what you did that precipitated your loss of discipline.

Discipline in trading is as simple as following your own trading rules and as complicated as the planning and preparation required, dealing with the fear of taking losses as well as profits, keeping careful records, and maintaining discipline as your top priority. Losses can be minimized only through discipline, and profits can be maximized only through discipline. As multifaceted and interdependent as the issue of discipline in trading is, ultimately it can be learned if commitment is strong enough. The rewards for discipline are the steady, day-by-day increases in profits from winning trades, and the inevitable reduction in drawdown and risk.

CHAPTER

12

Where Do You Go from Here?

Now that you have (hopefully) read what I've had to say about trading methods and trader psychology, you should have a very clear understanding of each area as well as their interactions. As you can clearly see, the odds of success in the stock market (or in any other market) are limited by trader psychology. While there are those who will tell you that the interaction of trader psychology and trading methodology is a complex topic that requires years of study and analysis, this is not the case. The facts are simple and undeniable. Investor psychology is the weakest link in the chain. Lack of discipline, inconsistent follow-through, failure to apply the rules of a trading system or method, and emotional responses to market behavior are the major reasons for trading losses. There is no system, method, timing indicator, or analytical approach to the markets that will not be undermined by these divisive forces.

If, after having read my many *caveats* and precautions, you are still not convinced that you need to have your "psychological house" in order before you attempt to apply the methods in this book (or, for that matter, any trading methods), then perhaps the cold reality of the markets will change your mind. It is my sincere hope and wish that you will heed my words of warning and that you will implement the many suggestions I have given with regard to discipline and trader psychology. Assuming you have taken my advice to heart, where should you go from here? My suggestions are given below.

- Study each of my strategies and make certain that you understand them clearly from start to finish. If, after having studied the methods to the best of your ability, you are still unclear about them, please send me an e-mail and I will do my best to assist you.

- Make absolutely certain that you understand and adhere to the rules of my GIM and STF. Of these, the STF is the most important. Every time you intend to make a trade, be certain it fits into the structure of the STF model. If it does not, then I urge you strongly to avoid making that trade since the odds of it being successful are fairly low.

- Remember that the "devil is in the details." By this I mean simply that for all of the methods discussed in the book, there are details that must be put into action at the right time and in the right sequence. You must use the correct types of orders for entry and for exit. You must use the right type of stop or stop-loss, and you must enter your orders at the right time. While these "housekeeping" details may seem trivial to you, I assure you that they are not. The success of your trading venture could easily rest upon the correct execution of these "minor" details. The best way to avoid having problems is by being organized and by following through according to the methods I have described for you.

- If you are in doubt about any of the procedures or methods then I urge you to avoid taking action. The old adage "when in doubt stay out" is *apropos*.

- "Do your own thing" is a well worn aphorism but it is certainly applicable to trading. As you well know, there are many opinions "out there" in the trading world. Some of these will run contrary to what your systems and methods are saying. Do not fall victim to these divergent opinions since they will only lead you astray.

- Test before you trade. Before you implement any of the strategies discussed in this book "try them on for size". By this I mean that not all strategies are right for all traders. Some strategies are too risky for some traders since they require a fairly large stop-loss. On the other hand, some of the methods discussed in this boom may be too tame for some traders. In addition to the degree of risk, the length of the trades may not be to your liking or they may not be consistent with your temperament. Some traders are unable to hold positions for more than a few days while other traders are loathe to hold trades for only a few days. You need to decide what's right for you. If a method or systems does not fit your personality or your style then you will be prone to implement it incorrectly or inconsistently, both of which will lead inevitable to losses.

- Do not over extend the size of your positions. In other words, do not trade too large a number of shares until you have gained confidence in the method or methods you are using.

Trading too large a position will cause you anxiety. Anxiety will cause you to make mistakes. Mistakes will cost you money. Mistakes will undermine your confidence. Lack of confidence will cause you to use your system inconsistently. And this will bring more losses.

- Expand your base of operations slowly and carefully. Once you have achieved success with these methods, you will have the confidence needed to increase the number of shares you are trading as well as the number of stocks you are trading. To expand your operations too quickly can be dangerous. But how will you know when to expand? A good rule of thumb is to trade more shares and more stocks when you have doubled your starting capital. In most cases it will take a good amount of time for you to arrive at this excellent spot, but the wait will be well worthwhile. Although you may have been told that it's good to be aggressive, I suggest that being aggressive at the wrong time can be very costly. Being an aggressive trader is good as long as your timing is right.

- And although last on my list, practice is by no means the least in importance. Learning the markets is like learning a new language. It takes time and practice. Market practice can consist of what has been called "paper trading" (pretend trading, or simulated trading). While such practice is a good thing, up to a point, beyond a given point practice will teach you nothing and it could, in fact, be deleterious to your ultimate goals. Why? Because simulated trading cannot replicate the emotional aspects and conditions that are part and parcel of the actual experience. It is not until your emotions have been tested that you will know how good or bad your discipline may be.

If I can be of assistance in your quest for stock market profits, please feel free to send me an e-mail. Although I cannot personally answer all the e-mails I receive, I try to respond to those that are in need of immediate attention. Either of the following addresses will come directly to me:

jake@trade-futures.com
jake@2chimps.com

I'm tempted to end with "good luck" as my closing statement; however, I believe that we are the masters of our own luck in the markets. Yes, it's true that a certain amount of good fortune can be helpful, but we must not allow ourselves to rely on luck or, for that matter, to believe in it. I will, therefore, end this book with the wish that you go forward with success using the methods I have taught you, since you alone are the architect of your market mastery.

—Jake Bernstein
Winnetka, Illinois

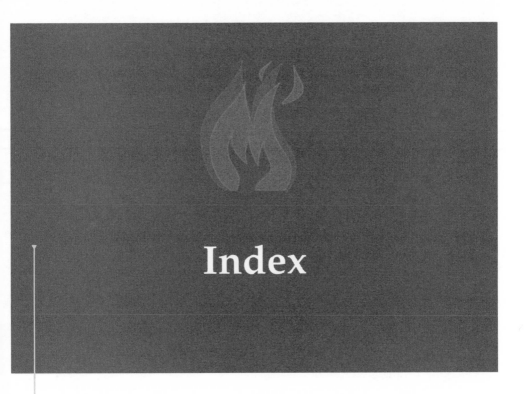

Index